Effective Careers Education & Guidance

Andrew Edwards
&
Anthony Barnes

Published by Network Educational Press Ltd.
PO Box 635
Stafford
ST16 1BF

First Published 1997
© Andrew Edwards & Anthony Barnes

ISBN 1 85539 045 0

Series Editor - Professor Tim Brighouse
Edited by Gina Walker
Design & layout by
Neil Hawkins of Devine Design
Illustrations by Barking Dog Art

Printed in Great Britain by
Redwood Books, Trowbridge, Wilts.

Foreword

A teacher's task is much more ambitious than it used to be and demands a focus on the subtleties of teaching and learning and on the emerging knowledge of school improvement.

This is what this series is about.

Teaching can be a very lonely activity. The time honoured practice of a single teacher working alone in the classroom is still the norm; yet to operate alone is, in the end, to become isolated and impoverished. This series addresses two issues – the need to focus on practical and useful ideas connected with teaching and learning and the wish thereby to provide some sort of an antidote to the loneliness of the long distance teacher who is daily berated by an anxious society.

Teachers flourish best when, in key stage teams or departments (or more rarely whole schools), their talk is predominantly about teaching and learning and where, unconnected with appraisal, they are privileged to observe each other teach; to plan and review their work together; and to practise the habit of learning from each other new teaching techniques. But how does this state of affairs arise? Is it to do with the way staffrooms are physically organised so that the walls bear testimony to interesting articles and in the corner there is a dedicated computer tuned to 'conferences' about SEN, school improvement, the teaching of English etc., and whether, in consequence, the teacher leaning over the shoulder of the enthusiastic IT colleague sees the promise of interesting practice elsewhere? Has the primary school cracked it when it organises successive staff meetings in different classrooms and invites the 'host' teacher to start the meeting with a 15 minute exposition of their classroom organisation and management? Or is it the same staff sharing, on a rota basis, a slot on successive staff meeting agenda when each in turn reviews a new book they have used with their class? And what of the whole school which now uses 'active' and 'passive' concerts of carefully chosen music as part of their accelerated learning techniques?

It is of course well understood that excellent teachers feel threatened when first they are observed. Hence the epidemic of trauma associated with OFSTED. The constant observation of the teacher in training seems like that of the learner driver. Once you have passed your test and can drive unaccompanied, you do. You often make lots of mistakes and sometimes get into bad habits. Woe betide, however, the back seat driver who tells you so. In the same way the new teacher quickly loses the habit of observing others and being observed. So how do we get a confident, mutual observation debate going? One school I know found a simple and therefore brilliant solution. The Head of the History Department asked that a young colleague plan lessons for her – the Head of Department – to teach. This lesson she then taught, and was observed by the young colleague. There was subsequent discussion, in which the young teacher asked,

"Why did you divert the question and answer session I had planned?"
and was answered by,
"Because I could see that I needed to arrest the attention of the group by the window with some "hands-on" role play, etc."

This lasted an hour and led to a once-a-term repeat discussion which, in the end, was adopted by the whole school. The whole school subsequently changed the pattern of its meetings to consolidate extended debate about teaching and learning. The two teachers claimed that because one planned and the other taught both were implicated but neither alone was responsible or felt 'got at'.

So there are practices which are both practical and more likely to make teaching a rewarding and successful activity. They can, as it were, increase the likelihood of a teacher surprising the pupils into understanding or doing something they did not think they could do rather than simply entertaining them or worse still occupying them. There are ways of helping teachers judge the best method of getting pupil expectation just ahead of self-esteem.

This series focuses on straightforward interventions which individual schools and teachers use to make life more rewarding for themselves and those they teach. Teachers deserve nothing less, for they are the architects of tomorrow's society, and society's ambition for what they achieve increases as each year passes.

Professor Tim Brighouse.

Acknowledgements

The authors would like to thank in particular the Tower Hamlets Education–Business Partnership and the School Time Enterprise Programme for allowing us to reproduce information from their publications.

Thanks also to Cambridgeshire Training and Development Ltd., and Cambridgeshire Careers Guidance Ltd. for permission to reproduce materials from the Cambridgeshire Careers Exchange project.

Contents

Section One	Scope and Value of Careers Education and Guidance	7
Section Two	The Needs of Students	15
Section Three	Careers Education	29
Section Four	Careers Guidance	47
Section Five	Working with Information	65
Section Six	Experiences of Work	77
Section Seven	Contributing to School Effectiveness and Improvement	85
Section Eight	The Role of the Careers Co-ordinator	93
Section Nine	Managing Staff Development in Careers Work	103
Section Ten	Schools and Careers Services in Partnership	113
Section Eleven	Networking and External Partnerships	125
Section Twelve	Ensuring Quality	131
Appendix		140
Bibliography		141

This symbol indicates that a table may be photocopied and enlarged for your own use without specific permission from the publishers.

He wishes for the cloths of heaven

Had I the heavens' embroidered cloths,
Enwrought with golden and silver light,
The blue and the dim and the dark cloths
Of night and light and the half-light,
I would spread the cloths under your feet:
But I, being poor, have only my dreams;
I have spread my dreams under your feet;
Tread softly because you tread on my dreams.

W. B. Yeats

The Scope and Value of Careers Education and Guidance

In Section One, we learn that:

☛ *Concepts of careers education and guidance are linked to the way in which careers and work are defined.*

☛ *Careers education and guidance, for the purposes of this book, are together defined as the planned provision of courses and activities to help young people manage their continuing personal and social development in the context of their choices of education, training and work.*

☛ *The proposed model of effective careers education and guidance focuses on meeting students' needs. It shows how this must be achieved through the provision that is made, and how, in turn, this provision needs to be managed and co-ordinated.*

The Meanings of 'Career' and 'Work'

'Career' and 'work' are the main organising concepts for defining the scope and value of careers education and guidance in the curriculum. It will be difficult to achieve agreement across the school about the scope and value of careers education and guidance unless staff have reached a consensus about the meanings of these terms. They are both complex, ambiguous and problematic concepts.

Work

'Work', at its broadest, refers to 'productive effort'. This sense of the term is important for justifying careers education and guidance in the curriculum of young people with severe learning difficulties, who may never be able to earn their own livelihood but who nevertheless need to be able to use their time productively. Equipping young people for working life, therefore, involves educating young people about paid jobs, voluntary work, unpaid work (including work as a student), work in the informal economy and work in the home. Inevitably, this will involve discussing with them the value, prestige and status attached to different kinds of work. As tomorrow's workers and citizens, young people need opportunities to reflect on how work is likely to be organised, experienced and rewarded in the future. Staff can help students by the appropriate use of:

- labour market information – incorporating data on current trends
- labour market intelligence – incorporating analysis and interpretation of current trends and future projections

Career

In everyday speech, we are likely to use the term 'career' in different ways, possibly even in the same sentence. A. G. Watts (1981) identified three common meanings of career, as exemplified in Table 1.1.

Table 1.1   Definitions of the term 'career'.

Definition (after Watts)	Example
Institutional	'a succession of related jobs, arranged in a hierarchy of prestige, through which persons move in an ordered (more-or-less predictable) sequence' *(Wilensky, 1961, quoted in Watts et al, 1981)*
Objective individual	'the sequence of positions through which the individual passes in the course of his working life' *(Watts et al, 1981)*
Subjective individual	'the moving perspective in which the person sees his life as a whole and interprets the meaning of his various attributes, actions and the things that happen to him' *(Hughes, 1937, quoted in Watts et al, 1981)*

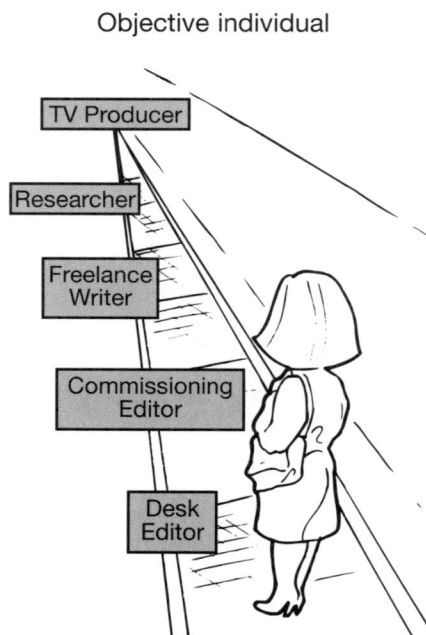

The key dimensions of these different definitions are:

- **control** – Who owns or determines a person's career? Is it the property of the individual or the institution?

- **interpretation** – Who makes sense of what has happened in a person's career? Is it the individual or others?

- **scope** – Who decides what is encompassed by 'career'? Is it just a person's paid work roles or can it include their unpaid work roles, and any or all of their life roles?

Effective Careers Education and Guidance

To a certain extent, the way in which we think about 'careers' today is influenced by continuing changes in work patterns and structures. In *Looking Forward* (1995), the School Curriculum and Assessment Authority (SCAA) defined 'career' as 'all aspects of an individual's evolving experience of work'. SCAA saw a career as belonging to, and being managed by, the individual. This equates with the current trend within organisations to make individuals responsible for managing their own careers. SCAA's emphasis on preparing young people to take control of this aspect of their lives increases the importance of personal and social learning and development at school.

Studies of changing career and work patterns suggest that young people in the future can expect to have many more changes of career than was formerly the case. Experience of rewarding and successful careers will depend much more than in the past on individuals investing in lifelong learning, to update and extend their skills. Jobs for life may have all but disappeared, but employability for life is still possible.

Kantner (1989, quoted in Collin, 1996) has identified the characteristics of four main types of career (Table 2.2). It is worth asking how well we are preparing students for these types of careers in the twenty-first century, assuming the continuation of present trends.

Table 2.2   Four main types of career (after Kantner, 1989)

Type of career	Key resource
bureaucratic	hierarchical position
professional	monopolisation of socially valued knowledge
entrepreneurial	capacity to create outputs
craft	practical skill

What is Careers Education and Guidance?

The way your school defines and values 'career' and 'work' will shape teachers' perceptions of careers education and guidance. Some staff may believe, for example, that you should give priority to preparing young people for paid employment and, therefore, pay little attention to other kinds of work. This section raises questions about whether such a narrow view is sufficient.

Similarly, some staff may still cling, consciously or sub-consciously, to an outmoded view of 'career'. Traditionally, 'careers' were largely the preserve of white middle class males in professional and managerial positions. If this view is retained, what does this mean for the careers education and guidance of women and of young people from ethnic minority backgrounds? How is the school helping young people to become everything that they can become? In some schools, often those with a traditional approach to careers education and guidance, careers work is, ironically, considered unnecessary for higher achievers, since it is assumed that they can manage without it.

As options in education, training and work increase, careers education and guidance becomes even more necessary. Far from being a peripheral activity, careers work should be at the core of the curriculum. Choosing satisfactory work is a vital ingredient of individual happiness, second only, perhaps, to our personal relationships.

The following definition attempts to capture a view of careers education and guidance which is sufficiently broad to be relevant, realistic and enriching for students, while remaining focused enough to provide clear direction and purpose for those responsible for developing careers programmes in schools.

> *Careers education and guidance is the planned provision of courses and activities to help young people manage their continuing personal and social development in the context of their choices of education, training and work.*

You may wish to adapt or amend this definition as you work through this book. It can be used to develop a model of effective careers provision. Such a model provides the structure for this book (Figure 1.1).

Figure 1.1 A model of effective careers provision.

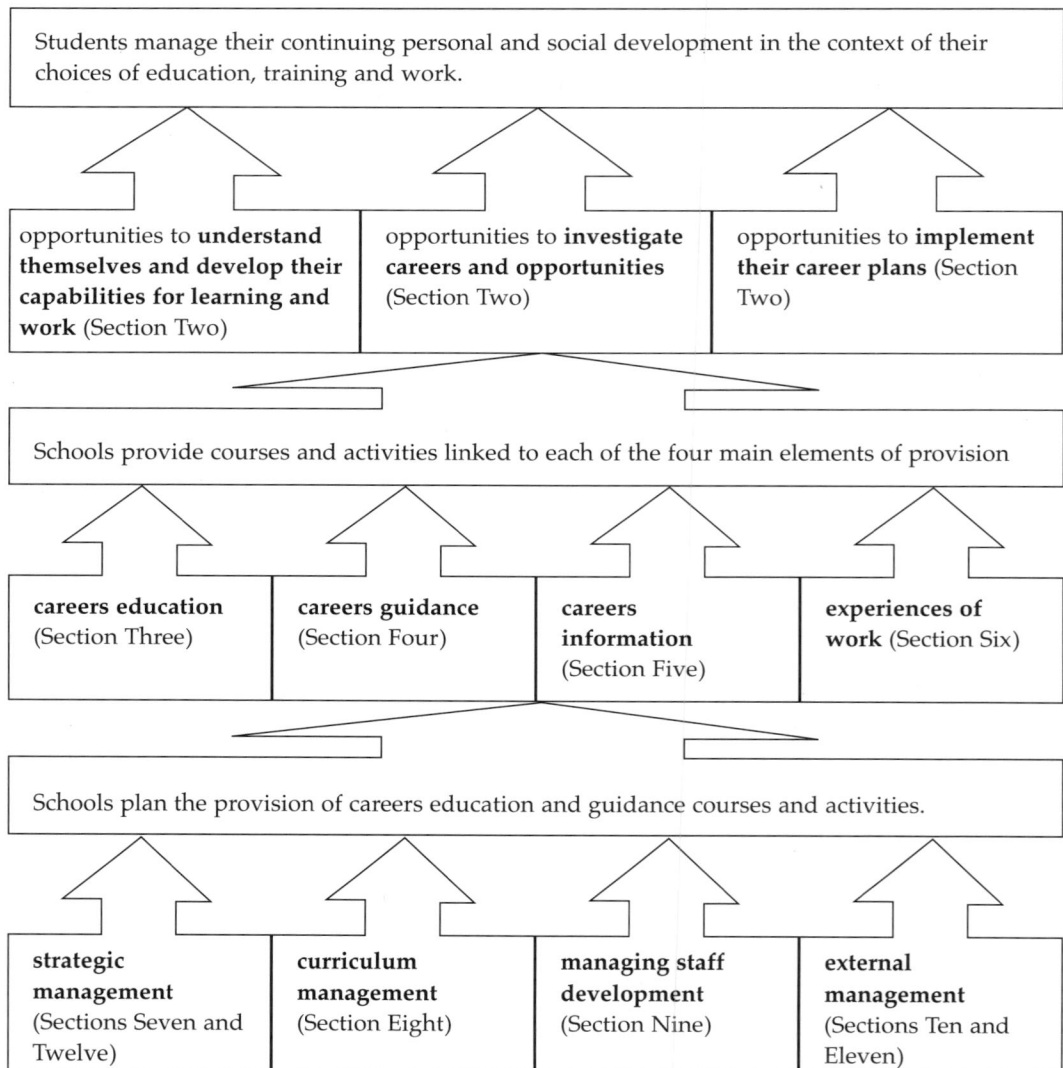

Students manage their continuing personal and social development in the context of their choices of education, training and work.

opportunities to **understand themselves and develop their capabilities for learning and work** (Section Two)

opportunities to **investigate careers and opportunities** (Section Two)

opportunities to **implement their career plans** (Section Two)

Schools provide courses and activities linked to each of the four main elements of provision

careers education (Section Three)

careers guidance (Section Four)

careers information (Section Five)

experiences of work (Section Six)

Schools plan the provision of careers education and guidance courses and activities.

strategic management (Sections Seven and Twelve)

curriculum management (Section Eight)

managing staff development (Section Nine)

external management (Sections Ten and Eleven)

Think about the learning opportunities that would be in keeping with the model of careers education and guidance described in Figure 1.1. Look at the activities suggested in Table 1.3 overleaf. Do you include any of these in your current careers programme? What changes would you make to meet the needs of your students?

Effective Careers Education and Guidance

Table 1.3 Activities that could form part of an effective careers programme.

Years 7 and and 8	• review how students coped with the primary–secondary school transition • meet the careers co-ordinator and link careers adviser, and visit the careers library • explore the main occupational groups • investigate issues at work e.g. equal opportunities, rights and responsibilities • develop career skills e.g. action-planning, target-setting, recording of achievement
Year 9	• investigate and make option choices • develop careers skills e.g. requesting help, using careers information, action-planning, negotiation, decision-making, recording of achievement • participate in a work-related activity e.g. industry day • prepare for part-time jobs e.g. personal finance education, understanding relevant employment laws
Years 10 and 11	• use a computer-assisted occupational interests program and an occupational or courses database • investigate labour market information and information about educational and training opportunities in relation to choices at 16+. • practise self-presentation skills e.g. letters of application, CVs, mock interviews • prepare for and participate in work-experience; and take part in a de-briefing activity • have a careers guidance interview or take part in a small group discussion • investigate and make choices related to options at 16+ • develop career skills e.g. requesting help, using careers information, action-planning, negotiation, decision-making, recording of achievement • attend careers convention or evening with parents
Years 12 and 13	• investigate issues relating to careers and work e.g. the future of work, the changing roles of women • use a computer-assisted occupational interests program and an occupational or courses database • investigate labour market information and information about educational and training opportunities in relation to choices at 17+ and 18+ • practise self-presentation skills e.g. letters of application, university/employer application forms, CVs, mock interviews • take part in appropriate work-related activities e.g. work-experience, mini enterprise, work-shadowing, industry days • have a careers guidance interview or take part in a small group discussion • investigate and make choices related to options at 17+ and 18+ • develop careers skills e.g. requesting help, using careers information, action-planning, negotiation, decision-making, recording of achievement

Planned Provision

As with all areas of curricular provision, careers education and guidance benefits from attention to breadth and balance, continuity and progression, differentiation and equality of opportunity.

The key elements in the management of the school's planned provision are:

- *Strategic management*
  e.g. policy-making and development planning, evaluating the impact of the careers provision on standards achieved

- *Curriculum management*
  e.g. developing schemes of work, devising curriculum guidelines

- *Managing staff development*
  e.g. organising training for staff, ensuring your own continuing professional development

- *'External' management*
  e.g. working with parents, developing education–business links, collaborating with the careers service

Courses and Activities

Students benefit from a mixture of opportunities that includes didactic, active, participative and experiential learning approaches. A range of teaching methods and activities, which encompasses individual, small-group and whole-class work, will foster independent and self-managed learning as well as co-operative learning. Personal careers guidance and support, including advice, information, counselling and advocacy, will help students to make choices wisely and responsibly.

The key elements in careers education and guidance are:

- *Careers education*
  This comprises the co-ordinated and progressive programme of teaching and learning activities provided for students in the curriculum, which will help them develop the knowledge and skills needed to manage their own careers.

- *Careers guidance*
  This comprises advice and guidance for individuals through interviews and small-group work, including participation in action-planning and recording-of-achievement activities, which will help students to implement their personal career plans.

- *Careers information*
  Comprehensive and reliable careers information, accessible to students of all abilities and ages, will help them to make well-informed and appropriate career choices and decisions.

- *Experiences of work*
  Learning about work first-hand will help students to develop their understanding of the meaning of work in people's lives, and of the skills that will be most useful to them. It can help them to test their ideas about work and to raise their awareness of opportunities that they might not otherwise have considered.

Personal and Social Development

A 'career' can be interpreted publicly (i.e. the pattern and sense that outsiders make of what has happened to others) as well as privately (i.e. the pattern and sense that individuals make of what has happened to them). As career patterns and structures continue to change, it is becoming even more important to empower individuals to interpret the meaning of work in their lives as a whole, and to manage their own careers. Increasingly, access to satisfying and rewarding careers will be for individuals who are prepared to invest in lifelong learning for lifelong career development.

The main outcomes that will equip young people for lifelong personal and social development can be related to three main priorities:

- helping students to understand themselves and develop their capabilities for learning and work
- helping students to investigate careers and opportunities
- helping students to implement their career plans

(based on Looking Forward, *SCAA, 1995)*

Action Points

☐ **Encourage discussion of the meanings of 'career' and 'work' among staff.**

☐ **Build a whole-school consensus on the value and importance of careers education and guidance.**

☐ **Use the model of effective careers provision (Figure 1.1) to review your school's current practice.**

☐ **Plan the best way for you to use this book – Figure 1.1 will help you decide the order in which you would like to work through the different Sections.**

Section Two

The Needs of Students

> *In Section Two, we learn that:*
>
> ☞ *Planning effective careers education and guidance provision depends on the accurate identification of students' needs.*
>
> ☞ *Career theories can inform our practice and help us to meet students' needs more effectively.*
>
> ☞ *Surveys of young people's attitudes can challenge our assumptions about students' needs and help us to improve careers education and guidance provision.*

Understanding the Needs of Students

Improving the effectiveness of your school's careers education and guidance provision depends on the accurate identification of your students' needs. Several theories attempt to explain students' career needs in childhood, early adolescence and through into adult life. Using such theories to inform practice can help to improve your school's provision. The results of large-scale, national surveys of young people's attitudes and views about careers and work can also be very helpful, although you should try to investigate the specific needs of your own students as well.

Students have psychological needs related to their inner well-being. Achieving high self-esteem and a positive self-concept helps students to make career choices, so activities to develop students' self-awareness are important. They need to be aware of their qualities, skills, aptitudes, interests, values and attitudes in relation to careers and work. In addition, students need to develop a range of personal skills including the abilities to compromise and make adjustments, to be self-reliant, to make decisions and to persevere (Table 2.1).

Table 2.1   Examples of activities to promote self-development.

Activity or skill	How activity could be achieved
self-assessment of qualities and skills	using checklists
receiving feedback from others	during paired work
reviewing own performance	as a member of a team
setting personal targets	negotiating targets with the tutor
recording achievements	maintaining a record of achievement folder
performing duties responsibly	helping at a parents' evening
showing initiative	organising a charity fund-raising event
being assertive, negotiating, making decisions	taking part in role plays and simulations

The concept of 'career maturity' is useful for describing students who have reached a stage of readiness to make career decisions and transitions. John Crites (1973) has developed an inventory for measuring students' career maturity. It identifies four main factors:

1. consistency of career choice
2. realism of career choice
3. competencies in choice and decision-making
4. maturity of attitude

Use the four headings from Crites' inventory to devise your own checklist of the behaviours and performances that you would expect from students – for example, at the end of each Key Stage and 16–19.

Using Career Theory

Kurt Lewin said that there was nothing quite as practical as a good theory! Theories suggest relationships and offer explanations and predictions of behaviour. Good theories provide useful perspectives, are easy to follow and make clear the limitations of their use. As teachers, we do need to draw on theory, in order to be aware of the ideas that underpin our actions. Some theories, such as those based on psychodynamic counselling, cannot be used unless the teacher is trained. Others might assume that the teacher has unlimited time to spend with each student. Clearly, the most relevant theories to careers teachers are those which can be applied successfully in a school setting. By combining theories that are compatible with each other, and which we find useful, we can improve our practice and meet students' needs more effectively.

In this book, it is possible only to provide a classification of career theories and a brief overview of some of the most influential theories on current practice. Over 120 career theories have been put forward so, not surprisingly, the boundaries of the classification are not watertight. Nevertheless, it does provide a useful starting point. For more information, please see more detailed sources (Seligman, 1994; Sharf, 1992; Watts et al, 1996).

Table 2.2 shows a classification of different types of career theory based on two dimensions:

1. the **discipline** from which the theory was derived. Psychological theories emphasise responses from within the individual. Sociological theories emphasise the individual's responses to external influences and controls.
2. the **situations** that the theory is attempting to explain. Structural theories deal with relatively static and controlled situations that might explain a student's choices and actions at a specific point in time. Process theories deal with changes and adjustments over time, such as those involved in decision-making and moving between stages of development.

Table 2.2 Types of career theory.

	Psychological	Sociological
Structural	● trait and factor (Parsons) ● congruence (Holland)	● opportunity structure (Roberts) ● accident
Process	● career development (Ginzberg, Super) ● circumscription–compromise (Gottfredson) ● career learning (Law)	● social learning (Krumboltz) ● community interaction (Law)

Trait and Factor

Trait and factor theories were the earliest to be developed in the careers field. The traits or characteristics of individuals are assessed so that they can be matched with the types of work that require those traits or characteristics. Parsons (1909) believed that tests can help individuals to understand their attitudes, abilities, interests, ambitions, resources and limitations, and their causes. Occupational information can give individuals knowledge of the requirements and conditions of success, advantages and disadvantages, compensations, opportunities, and the prospects in different lines of work. By a process of 'true reasoning' of the relations between these two groups of factors, individuals can make career choices.

> Think about how you use the trait and factor approach in your own careers work. How can you guard against using this approach in too mechanistic a way? How can you help your students to benefit from this way of thinking? (For example, students could devise questionnaires for other students to try out.)

Congruence

The trait and factor approach has been highly developed by John Holland (1966). His theory of 'occupational personality' is based on six types of people who correspond to six occupational environments. Individuals seek work environments that are 'congruent' with their personalities (Table 2.3 and Figure 2.1). In practice, people and work environments are made up of combinations of types.

Table 2.3 Types of occupational personalities and environments, according to a 'congruence' career theory.

Realistic	involves practical or problem-solving behaviour, physical activities requiring skill, strength and co-ordination (examples: forestry, farming, construction)
Investigative	involves abstract and critical thinking (examples: science, mathematics, computer programming)
Artistic	involves self-expression, artistic creation, expression of emotions and individualistic activities (examples: art, music, education)
Social	involves using verbal and social skills to help people (examples: teaching, speech therapy, social work)
Enterprising	involves using verbal activities to persuade, manage and lead (examples: management, sales work, politics)
Conventional	involves being dependable and having the ability to follow rules and orders (examples: accounting, book-keeping)

Figure 2.1 Psychological resemblance among types of occupational personalities.

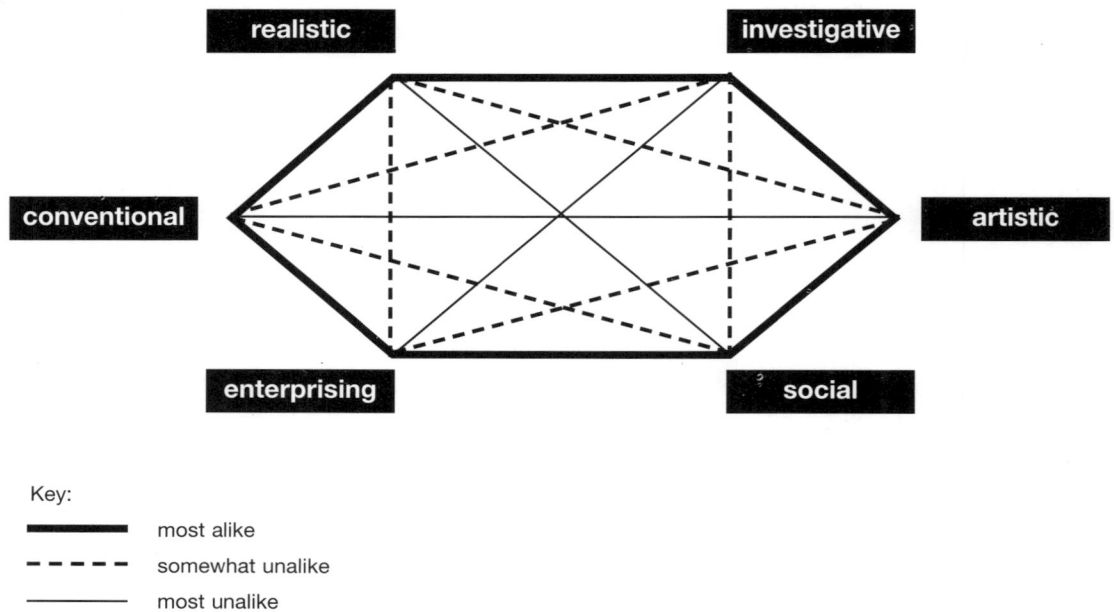

Key:

——————— most alike

– – – – – somewhat unalike

—————— most unalike

> Look at published materials based on the congruence approach to see if they could be used to strengthen your careers programme. Examples include Holland's *Self-Directed Search* (Psychological Assessment Resources Inc.) and the *Odyssey* program (Progressions Ltd.).

Career Development

Trait and factor approaches are useful when you need to help an individual to make career choices at a particular moment in time; but you may have contact with your students over 6 or 7 years in a secondary school. Theories that help to explain career choice and development throughout childhood, adolescence and into adult life would be useful in the longer term. Such career development theories are primarily about how individuals build their identity and self-image based on their own perceptions and the perceptions of others.

Career development theories can be usefully combined with trait and factor approaches to support careers work in schools. Career development theory, for example, can provide a basic map for charting the learning and development of students as they move through and beyond school; and trait-and-factor approaches can be used effectively at specific career decision-points.

Ginzberg (1951) identified three main stages of career development (Table 2.4).

Table 2.4   Stages in career development (after Ginzberg).

Fantasy	up to age 11	individuals use play and imagination in thinking about work roles	
Tentative	age 11 to 17	The sub-stages are:	
		interest	individuals clarify their likes and dislikes
		capacity	individuals assess their own abilities
		value	individuals consider their values
		transition	individuals face up to the need to make career decisions
Realistic	age 17+	The sub-stages are:	
		exploration	individuals explore and find out about a wide variety of adult roles
		crystallisation	individuals become more focused
		specification	individuals make a specific choice in a deliberate, systematic and realistic way

Ginzberg's stages (Table 2.4) can help you to assess students' career maturity and their readiness to make decisions. Super's (1990) life-span theory proposes similar stages but also includes the later stages of life (Table 2.5).

Table 2.5   Stages in career development according to a life-span theory (after Super).

Growth	birth to age 14	Children develop some awareness of their personal interests and capabilities. They imagine what they would like to do and become; and towards the end of this stage, they start to think about what is realistic and likely.
Exploration	age 15 to 24	This is a time of intense self-discovery and growing independence. Individuals assess and re-assess their interests, abilities and values. They find out about opportunities and are exposed to various sources of influence and information. Individuals move closer to a realistic concept of their preferred occupational roles.
Establishment	age 25 to 44	Individuals establish a more stable pattern of work that suits them. There may still be some experimentation, but movement is closely associated with promotion and changing jobs.
Maintenance	age 45 to 64	Individuals consolidate their careers. This can be either a period of self-fulfilment, if goals have been achieved, or a period of frustration, if individuals feel unfulfilled.
Decline	age 65+	Individuals react differently to this stage. Some re-assess their interests, abilities, values and opportunities, and choose new kinds of learning and work. Others do not recover from a sense of loss of identity.

Changing career patterns and structures at the end of the twentieth century suggest that some parts of Super's theory may not be quite so relevant. This could provide an interesting focus for a discussion with students. Possible questions include:

- Do these stages adequately describe the typical career experiences of women?
- Do the stages of Establishment and Maintenance need to be re-defined? (This should raise students' awareness of issues such as greater instability, career changing, redundancy and contract working.)
- Should the last stage be re-defined? ('Career re-focusing' has been suggested in place of 'career decline'.)

Circumscription–Compromise

Gottfredson's (1981) circumscription–compromise theory is compatible with Super's life-span theory, but is particularly interesting for its emphasis on career development in childhood and early adolescence. Gottfredson offers an explanation of how individuals limit their consideration of the full range of options and how they approach the compromises or adjustments they need to make if they have to re-assess their options (Table 2.6).

Table 2.6   Stages in career development in childhood and early adolescence (after Gottfredson).

Stage 1	age 3 to 5	The distinction between magical or illusory things and real things is understood.
Stage 2	age 6 to 8	The distinction between male and female is understood. Identification with own-sex roles and exclusion of opposite-sex roles occurs.
Stage 3	age 9 to 13	Distinctions of class and occupational prestige are understood. Influence of social class and peer group is felt on individual's aspirations.
Stage 4	age 14+	Orientation to 'internal unique self' occurs. Individuals make choices that are compatible with the view of themselves they want to project and develop.

Gottfredson's work is significant in demonstrating the relevance of careers education and guidance in the primary curriculum. It also helps teachers to focus on gender issues and the need to challenge stereotyping explicitly as well as sensitively.

Think about your own early career ideas, the influences on your choices and the adjustments you made to ensure that your decisions were realistic. What insights could your students gain from this kind of thinking?

Effective Careers Education and Guidance

Career Learning

Several theorists attempt to explore the nature of career learning. Bill Law's career learning theory (1996) is discussed in more detail in Section Five.

> **How could you use career learning theory to improve the planning and design of careers lessons?**

Social Learning

Krumboltz (1979) based his approach to career decision-making on social learning theory. He identified four main influences on individuals:

1. inherited attributes and abilities
2. environmental conditions and events
3. learning experiences
4. task-approach skills

Students' overall education, which may include careers education and guidance, plays a part in shaping these influences. According to Krumboltz, these learning processes interact to produce three major types of outcomes:

1. self-observation generalisations
2. task-approach skills (task-approach skills are outcomes as well as influences)
3. actions (the individual's career-related actions are the result of the previous two outcomes)

> **The issues raised by social learning theory are particularly rich. On the matter of task-approach skills, think about how you and your students approach an impending decision. Work on decision-making with students often focuses on the point of decision itself, but how could you improve students' ability to be successful decision-makers in the long term?**

Community Interaction

Law's (1981) community interaction theory also explains career development in terms of person–environment interactions. Interpersonal exchanges and interactions within the individual's local community have a significant impact on his or her career development. Law provides one of the strongest arguments for planned and progressive experiences of work as part of the careers education and guidance programme. Students' encounters, attachments and networks can have both liberating and entrapping effects: positive liaisons and experiences should be encouraged in order to release students from the restrictive influences of other attachments.

> **How could you harness the power of community-linked work in your careers programme to strengthen the benefits to students? Conversely, how can you guard against the possibility of such work having negative effects?**

Opportunity Structure

Roberts (1977) offered a more sobering perspective and sparked off a passionate debate about the effectiveness of careers education and guidance. Roberts claimed that opportunity structure rather than occupational choice is the principal determinant of how people enter different kinds of work. Careers practitioners have little influence because educational attainment, home and family background, and the economic and social structure, override individual choice factors. This theory could help careers teachers to think about the possible limits of their roles and the extent to which they should challenge or collude with the prevailing economic and social structure.

While Roberts' original theory cast doubt on the usefulness of careers education and guidance, he has recently argued that there is now more scope for effective intervention by careers practitioners (see Section Eight). This is because, as a result of changes in youth participation rates in education, in training and in the labour market, students are facing a more prolonged transition in the search for an adult career identity, during which careers guidance has more time to be effective.

The oral history tradition can provide a rich source of evidence of the constraints of the opportunity structure in the early and mid-twentieth century. Ask your students to interview their grandparents about this, if possible. Also encourage students to find and discuss newspaper articles and TV programmes which draw attention to continuing inequalities today.

Accident Theory

Accident theory raises the issue of how chance factors affect what happens to individuals in their careers. Students may meet someone, volunteer for an activity or take a part-time job with very little real planning and yet that event becomes highly significant for them. For careers teachers, this is a reminder that an excessively rational approach to career planning is unrealistic and that schools need to help students review and reflect on chance events.

What are the strengths and limitations of accident theory? Does accident theory undermine the place of careers education and guidance in schools?

This overview of some influential career theories has not done justice to the richness of the ideas and explanations; but hopefully it has shown how theory can help you to address students' needs.

Using Surveys of Young People

Surveys are an important source of information about young people's changing attitudes and ideas in relation to themselves and the worlds of learning and work. By following up published reports of national studies, you can find out what young people generally feel about themselves and their career circumstances. You can also use action research to ask your students about their needs directly.

Four examples of recent surveys are described on the following pages, and issues for careers teachers to consider are suggested.

Factors Influencing Option Choices with Reference to Later Career Choice
Ruth Frith and Pat Mahony (Roehampton Institute, London, June 1995)

This project investigated the factors influencing girls' and boys' option choices in Year 9, with reference to career choice post 16. It involved 128 students in three Essex schools. Key findings included the following.

- Schools promote a broad and balanced curriculum to maximise future education and employment opportunities. However, some students reject this and would prefer either to specialise early or to pursue their subject preferences.

- There is evidence that subject preference is still gendered. However, forcing students to study subjects they do not like is no guarantee that they will learn to like them or that they will want to continue with them post 16 (even though they may achieve).

- For many, the teacher remains a significant influence on whether a student likes a subject, succeeds with it and chooses it at Key Stage 4 and beyond.

- The research highlights the importance of students' families and parents, in particular of the mother, in the process of making option choices. GNVQs appear to be more popular with pupils and teachers than with parents.

- Many students reported that members of their families are employed in traditionally gendered occupations. In the light of the knowledge that family members have a particular influence in subject and career choice, it is likely that students will continue to be influenced by stereotyping unless specific strategies are adopted to address this issue.

- In some cases, girls and boys hold different views about their control over potential self-improvement. Although a number of girls and boys stated that improvements can be made if they work hard at a subject, many – in particular boys – said they think that some subjects are 'easier for girls' or 'easier for boys' because of natural ability. Some boys also believe that they have little chance to overcome this by hard work.

- The expectations of many of the students are limited and unrealistic, and they are unclear about their future aspirations and their abilities.

What implications do these findings have for your partnership with parents and your option choice process?

Opportunity and Disadvantage at Age 16
Ann Hagell and Catherine Shaw (Policy Studies Institute, London, 1996)

This research investigated the destinations and experiences of disadvantaged young people as they reached the end of their compulsory schooling. It was based on a survey of 3000 inner city 16-year-olds from 34 schools within six urban areas of England. The key findings are summarised below.

- The sample achieved fewer GCSEs at higher grades than would be expected according to national figures. Chinese and Indian respondents achieved the highest scores.

- Sessions with the local careers service were rated as the most useful source of careers advice, in preference to school-based services.

- Three-quarters of the sample continued in full-time education at 16+. These respondents were the happiest with their choice, but in many cases they experienced money problems and debt. The report concludes that it is very important that the content of the education received by this group is specifically tailored for the type of job market they will have to enter at some point.

- 11% of the sample chose some full-time study during the course of the year, alongside other activities. Black respondents typically underwent one month of training. Training can be the least positive option, particularly if it is not employer-based. This group reported more pressures and problems during the year.

- 15% of the sample chose activities other than studying, for the whole year. This option was more likely for white respondents than for other ethnic groups. Those in full-time work were happy with their choice.

- The report concludes that careers guidance professionals must play a role in ensuring that the most potentially vulnerable young people are directed to suitable courses with realistic aims.

What implications do these findings have for the design of Year 11 careers programmes?

Job Ambitions of the Next Generation
(City & Guilds MORI Survey Report, 1995)

This survey investigated the career aspirations of teenagers and their parents, and the influences on these aspirations. It involved 1198 face-to-face interviews with 15- to 18-year-olds. Key findings included the following.

- *'These days, it is just as important for a woman to get a good job as for a man.'* Only half of the male young people surveyed strongly agreed with this statement. This compares with 4 out of 5 of the young women.

- *'I don't mind what job I have as long as it's well paid.'* The three most important career choice motivators among young people are a well-paid job (39%), which is challenging and interesting (37%), and which has good career prospects (31%). Young men are especially motivated by money (46%) and job security is more important to them than to young women (29% v 13%).

- *'I do not expect to have an interesting job.'* 77% of young adults *do* expect to have an interesting job.

- *'I will need qualifications to get a good job.'* Almost all young people agreed with this statement. 82% expect to continue to learn after they have left formal education.

How well do young people understand the current state of the labour market?

How realistic are their expectations of adult working life?

What implications does this survey have for the content of your school's careers programme?

Working lives in the 1990s

Alan Hudson, Dennis Hayes and Toby Andrew (Global Futures, 1996)

This report set out the provisional findings of the Attitudes to Work Survey, which was based on 1000 interviews with 18- to 65-year-olds in employment, in 15 geographical areas. The key findings are summarised below.

- 52% of under-25s said the main reason they work is to earn money for basic essentials such as food, rent and mortgage, compared to an average of 67% for those over 25.

- 54% of under-25s said they feel involved in decision-making in their present job.

- 39% of under-25s identified education and training as the best way of advancing their careers.

- under-25s said that they socialise fortnightly with colleagues outside of working hours, on average. The pub is the favourite venue.

- 32% of under-25s said that they feel personally responsible for the work they do but only occasionally feel the job is worth doing.

- under-25s are less likely to expect an annual pay rise (34% compared to 58% of those over 25). 26% of under-25s compete for performance-related increments.

- 87% of under-25s said that they had to work extra hours in the workplace.

- under-25s specified the following as the biggest problems at work: poor pay, management relations, workloads, hours.

- 24% of under-25s belong to a trade union compared with over 50% of those aged 35 and over.

Do you think these results show that young people feel pessimistic or optimistic about their experiences of working life?

Are you surprised by any of the findings?

How could you use some of this data with your students?

How Can Schools Use Research and Surveys?

Try the following suggestions to help you use the findings of research and surveys more effectively:

- **Disseminate** findings to colleagues and others.
- **Re-assess** the extent to which your curriculum meets students' needs.
- **Re-define** the purpose of careers education and guidance in the curriculum, if necessary, in order to establish new priorities.

Action Points

☐   **Identify the particular needs of the students in your school.**

☐   **Decide on how you can make the best use of career theory to support your work.**

☐   **Make a point of looking for articles about career theory and surveys of young people; and follow them up appropriately.**

Section Three

Careers Education

In Section Three, we learn that:

☞ **The development of a successful careers education and guidance programme requires schools to be clear about what they want students to learn and how they can help students to learn more effectively.**

☞ **Effective curriculum management of careers education and guidance is linked to the development and use of a policy statement, entitlement statements, a development plan, audits, curriculum guidelines, schemes of work, lesson plans and evaluation reports.**

Getting the Most out of Careers Education

How can we maximise the learning gains for students from the range of activities in the careers programme? This issue does not always get the attention it deserves. School accountability is currently fixated on league tables of exam results rather than on equipping young people for careers that are personally rewarding, and which contribute to the well-being of others.

The issue also presents a number of challenges. Careers provision is often fragmented and diffuse, making it difficult to maintain a momentum of learning. Assessment of students' career learning is problematic since one does not wish to label individuals as failures. In this Section, we will look at:

● what students need to learn
● how we can help students to learn
● how we can assess and accredit what students have learned in appropriate ways

What Students Need to Learn
Table 3.1 summarises the main learning opportunities that schools may wish to provide, as suggested in *Looking Forward* (SCAA, 1995).

Table 3.1 Aims of careers education and guidance at Key Stages 3 and 4 (KS3, KS4), and Post 16 (P16).

I: Students understand themselves and develop their capabilities	II: Students investigate careers and opportunities	III: Students implement their career plans
Students should be given opportunities to:		
consider their own qualities and skills (KS3) assess their personal qualities and skills (KS4, P16)	investigate the knowledge and skills that people need at work (KS3) investigate the knowledge and skills that people need at work and the methods used to assess these (KS4, P16)	make decisions concerning their own learning and curriculum (KS3) make decisions concerning their own post 16 choices (KS4) develop effective strategies for making and implementing decisions (P16)
reflect on their interest for particular work roles and activities (KS3) clarify and discuss their values, attitudes and preferences in relation to work (KS4, P16)	use occupational and labour market information to investigate opportunities (KS3, KS4, P16)	use action-planning and the recording of achievement to support their career development (KS3, KS4, P16)
develop key skills and capabilities (KS3, KS4, P16)	investigate social and moral issues in careers and work (KS3, KS4, P16)	seek and use information and guidance to support their career development (KS3, KS4, P16)
develop career management skills, including self-reliance and self-presentation (KS3, KS4, P16)	consider changing patterns of work and careers (KS3, KS4) develop critical awareness of the changing nature of work and careers (P16)	use the results of self-assessment in their career planning (KS4, P16)
	develop ways of organising information about work (KS3, KS4, P16)	
	find out about post 16 choices of education, training and work (KS4)	
	find out about opportunities in further and higher education, training and work, including employment and self-employment (P16)	
	explore the personal, social and economic value of work (P16)	

Effective Careers Education and Guidance

Helping Students to Learn

As a careers teacher, you should be aware of the main influences on how and what students learn. The model illustrated in Figure 3.1 shows the complex interactions in a learning situation.

Figure 3.1 A model of learning in careers education and guidance (adapted from Biggs and Moore, 1993).

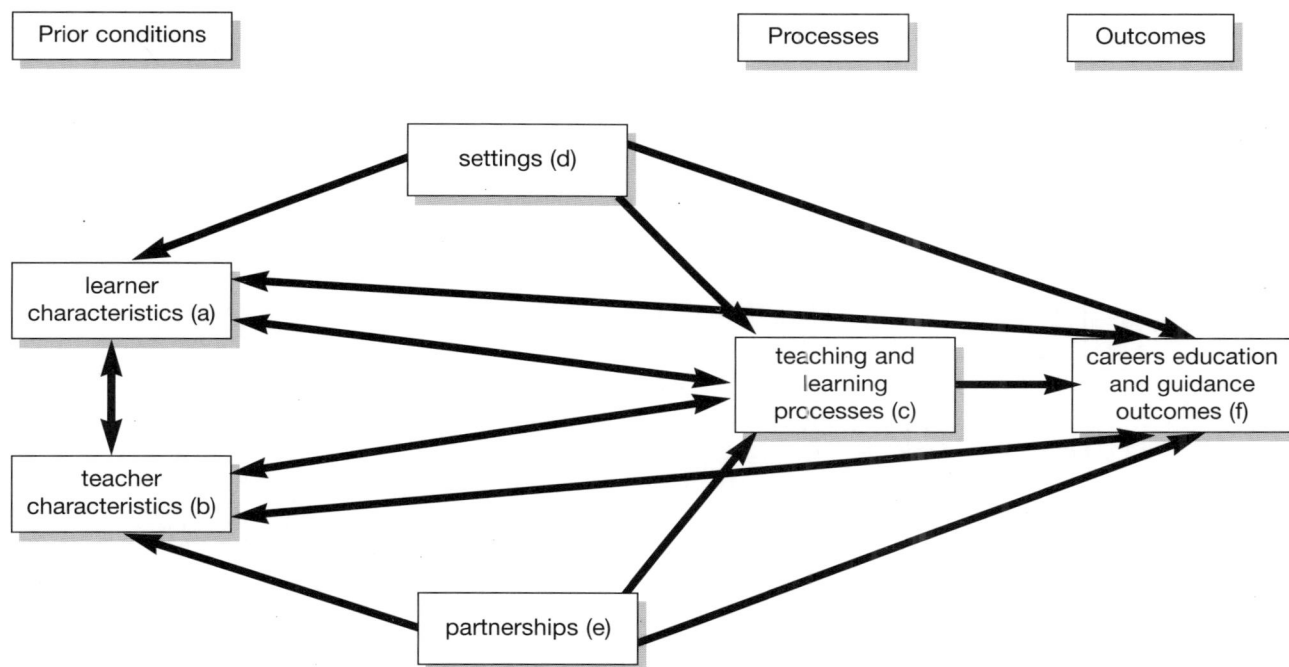

(a) Learner characteristics

What students can learn is influenced by their capacities (e.g. talents and aptitudes, health circumstances, and special educational needs), preferred learning styles, stage of career development and level of motivation.

One of the most interesting attempts to analyse different capacities is Howard Gardner's theory of multiple intelligences (1983). Particular 'frames of mind' are associated with specific career talents (see Table 3.2).

Table 3.2 Association of 'frames of mind' with career talents, according to Gardner's theory of multiple intelligences.

'Frame of mind'	Career talent
bodily-kinaesthetic	gymnasts and dancers
musical	composers and performers
linguistic	poets and writers
logico-mathematical	scientists and mathematicians
spatial	architects and artists
interpersonal	skilled negotiators
intrapersonal	mystics

Opportunities for careers education and guidance occur both informally and formally. Everyday learning is influenced by parents, the peer group and the media, and by students' part-time jobs. Some of the defining moments in a person's career may be the results of serendipity or 'happenstance'. Formal providers need to recognise and build on their students' informal learning in everyday situations.

(b) Teacher characteristics
Different teachers bring different expertise, experience and enthusiasm to careers work. The quality of the teacher's relationship with students has a major impact on what students learn.

(c) Teaching and learning processes
The issue of how to select appropriate teaching and learning strategies can be explored by looking at five of the most common situations or activities in careers programmes, as outlined in Table 3.3.

Table 3.3 Activities or situations for which different teaching and learning strategies are appropriate.

Activity or situation	Example
a decision-point	e.g. choices at 13+, 16+, 17+ and 18+
a work-related activity	e.g. work-experience, work-shadowing, mini enterprise
an investigation	e.g. careers using biology, careers in multimedia
a self-evaluation activity	e.g. Kudos or ISCOM
a skill-development activity	e.g. mock interviews (self-presentation and negotiation)

'Fitness for purpose' is the most important criterion when choosing methods and strategies for teaching. Constraints of time, resources and money may also affect decisions about the most desirable teaching and learning processes. Use the activity described on the next page to help you reflect on the effectiveness of three organisational approaches and three teaching-and-learning methods in each of the five situations outlined in Table 3.3.

Activity

Organisational approaches:

- individualised – individual works on his or her own
- co-operative – collaborative or team work in small groups
- whole-class – the full class is taught and learns together

Teaching-and-learning methods:

- didactic – exposition or instruction; question-and-answer sessions
- active/participative – students work actively on practical tasks and projects
- experiential – students learn from 'doing', such as role play, simulation and workplace activities

In the grid below, code each of the five common careers education situations using one of these symbols:

✓✓   = highly effective to use this type of organisation or method in this situation

✓   = quite effective

?   = not sure

0   = generally not effective

Situation	Organisational approach			Teaching-and-learning methods		
	individualised	co-operative	whole class	didactic	active/ participative	experiential
a decision-point						
a work-related activity						
an investigation						
a self-evaluation activity						
a skill-development activity						

This activity shows that we often have a choice in the organisational arrangements and methods we use, and that we need to take into account the preferences and natural styles of individual teachers and students. It also shows that teachers involved in careers work must be prepared to use a full and balanced range of approaches.

(d) Settings

Learning about careers is not confined to the classroom. Valuable learning can be organised in workplace settings for students doing work-experience. Simulated workplace settings can also be set up in schools and colleges.

(e) Partnerships

Students can benefit greatly from the involvement of careers guidance professionals. Adults-other-than-teachers (AOTs) can enhance students' learning by working alongside them as advisers, mentors, working coaches or supervisors.

(f) Careers education and guidance outcomes

The achievement of learning outcomes for students is related to the prior conditions and processes in the learning model. It is useful to distinguish between intended and actual outcomes. Intended outcomes are part of the objectives set at the planning stage. When writing outcome statements you need to specify:

- the **behaviour or action** e.g. select..., distinguish..., evaluate...
- the **careers context or situation** e.g. self-understanding, options at 16+
- the **standard of performance** e.g. at the right time, to meet employers' requirements

Evaluation helps to check the extent of any gaps or differences between intended and actual outcomes.

Assessing Students' Learning

Assessment is measuring what students have learned through the careers programme. It can be linked with accreditation to provide a means of recognising students' achievement.

It is important to be clear why you want to assess students' career learning and development. Table 3.4 summarises the key arguments for and against assessment.

Table 3.4 Arguments for and against assessment of career learning.

For	Against
we should not take it for granted that the careers programme is benefiting students	we do not want to fail young people just starting out in their careers
assessment helps us find out with some degree of precision how students are benefiting	we may neglect wider aspects of careers work in order to prepare students for assessment
assessment helps us to work out what students need to learn next	assessment may be too resource intensive

Decisions have to be made about when to assess students' career learning in the light of these arguments. Unnecessary and inappropriate assessment can take the enjoyment out of careers work for students. Effective assessment is linked to clear purposes:

- **summative assessment** – e.g. at the end of a careers course to check what students have learned
- **formative assessment** – e.g. to provide students and teachers with relevant information at a career decision-point
- **diagnostic assessment** – e.g. to identify what students need to learn next

Schools have access to a range of different approaches to assessment. 'Fitness for purpose' is a key consideration. This will help you decide which approach to use. If you are seeking students' perceptions of what they have learned, the information you gain may be highly subjective. If you wish to make comparisons across a large student cohort, you may need to use a more objective assessment tool. Assessment often involves taking care not to make generalisations or excessive claims about what you have found out.

Examples of assessment techniques, which can be used singly or in combination, include:

1. Psychometric tests and inventories
e.g. The Morrisby Profile. This provides a comprehensive picture of individual aptitudes, personality and other personal characteristics, which can be used in the guidance process to help students with their career choices and decisions.

2. Questions
Table 3.5 shows some examples of questions that could be used in the context of assessment.

Table 3.5   Some assessment questions.

Area	Question
self-awareness	What did you learn about yourself?
opportunity awareness	What did you learn about the first destinations of last year's Year 11 students?
decision-learning	What did you learn about making decisions?
transition-learning	What did you learn about coping when your work situation changes?

3. Unfinished sentences
Table 3.6 shows some examples of sentence-completion exercises that could be used for assessment.

Table 3.6   Some sentence-completion exercises for assessment.

Area	Unfinished sentence
self-awareness	'I was good at...'
opportunity awareness	'I found out about Modern Apprenticeships from...'
decision-learning	'The steps I went through in making my decision were...'
transition-learning	'I prepared for my university admissions interview by...'

4. Self-assessment tickboxes

Variants on the simple 'Yes/No' tickbox include:

- graded statements

e.g. action-planning:

Can write a simple action plan involving 3–6 steps, for the completion of a careers task (e.g. investigating options at 13+), with appropriate help	Can maintain and review an action plan, seeing it through to completion	Can create and maintain a comprehensive careers action plan, amending it and reviewing it as necessary (e.g. a Key Stage 4 or Post 16 plan)	Can identify when action-planning could be beneficial, can create plans without outside help and use them effectively
✓	✓	✓	

- rating scales

e.g. transition learning:

Getting to my work-experience placement by public transport

	very well	quite well	OK	not very well	not well at all
'I did this...'	✓				

- ranking scales

e.g. options:

Which activities did you learn most from in the Year 9 options module? Please rank them on a scale of 1 ('I learned a lot') to 6 ('I learned a little').

Activity	Rank order
Reading the school's options booklet	4
Listening to Heads of Department explaining what is involved in taking the subjects they teach	5
Making a Year 9 options action plan	3
Discussing how to choose with students from Year 10	1
Talking to my tutor on my own about my options	2
Watching the *Which Way Now* video	6

- validity checks

e.g. asking someone who has worked alongside the student to fill out the boxes and comparing this assessment with the student's own assessment of themselves.

e.g. asking students to record whether they did what they did on their own, with some help, or with a lot of help. This can be very useful for measuring progress for special needs students whose learning steps may be very small.

5. Multiple choice items

The example below shows part of a multiple choice assessment item focusing on opportunity awareness in the context of part-time jobs.

Question 1

Which of the following rules apply to jobs such as cleaning cars, gardening and baby-sitting, which you can do at any age for family and friends who are not in business?

MARK 3 ANSWERS

- ❏   A   You can do these sorts of jobs as often as you like, provided that you do not take time off school.
- ❏   B   You are allowed to accept payment.
- ❏   C   You cannot work before 7 a.m. or after 7 p.m. on any day.
- ❏   D   It is up to the adult to decide if you are sufficiently responsible to do the job.

6. Individual interviews and focus groups

Interviewing individuals or groups to find out what they have learned is a skilled activity which requires an understanding of:

- types of questioning
- effective listening
- ways of recording, analysing and interpreting information
- managing the dynamics of the situation

7. Assessed portfolio

Portfolio-based assessment is a relevant and appropriate way of assessing students' career learning, especially when it is integrated with other support processes in the school such as recording achievements. Students assemble a selection of 'evidence' of their careers planning activity over a period such as a Key Stage. Evidence of career learning and development can be presented in a variety of forms, including documentation, photographs or tapes. The portfolio is a distillation of what the school has tried to do for the student through its careers education and guidance programme. You can help your students by suggesting ways of structuring their portfolios (see Figure 3.2).

Figure 3.2 A suggested format for a career learning portfolio.

Opening statement	personal details
Timeline	summary of key events and activities during the period that the portfolio has been maintained
Self-evaluation materials	e.g. annotated examples of printouts from computer-assisted guidance programs, skills profiles, etc.
Action plans	e.g. current and completed action plans covering decision and transition points such as choices at 16+
Consultation notes	e.g. records of discussions held with adult helpers such as tutors, mentors, careers teachers and careers advisers
Diaries and logs	e.g. records of participation in events and activities such as work-experience and work-shadowing
Investigations	examples of research into choices and opportunities
Certificates	examples of awards, such as the Youth Award Scheme, which indicate achievement in careers-related areas
Other information	other relevant materials that the student wishes to include
Reflective commentary	a final statement by the student saying where he/she is now in the career planning process and explaining the significance of the particular pieces of evidence that have been selected for inclusion in the portfolio

The criteria to be used in assessing students' portfolios need to be clear. The criteria set out in Table 3.7 are based on 'FIRST', a mnemonic developed by Tol Bedford (1982).

Table 3.7 Criteria for assessing career learning portfolios. The student displays the following characteristics, commensurate with his/her age and ability.

Focus	the student has a clear sense of direction and purpose
Information	the student is well-informed about the opportunities he/she is considering
Realism	the student has realistically high aspirations based on an awareness of his/her own capabilities, circumstances and the availability of opportunities
Scope	the student is aware of alternative opportunities and is open-minded and flexible enough to consider them should it become necessary
Tactics	the student knows how to prepare, plan and take the necessary steps to implement his/her career ideas

The criteria listed in Table 3.7 could be applied by an informed adult such as a governor, local employer or teacher, following a discussion with the student about his/her career learning portfolio. Such a person could give the student valuable written feedback on what they have achieved so far, and suggest future areas for growth and development.

Effective Careers Education and Guidance

Recognising Students' Achievements

Recognition schemes have resource implications that need to be considered.

Schools that already record achievements may wish to broaden the scope of what they do to record and recognise students' career learning and development. If the process can be validated through an accreditation scheme, its value may be enhanced.

Existing accreditation schemes, such as those listed below, make it possible to assess particular aspects of career learning.

- **Life skills** – AEB Basic Tests, Welsh Board Certificate of Education, Youth Award Scheme, RSA Initial Award in life skills. (These schemes are particularly suitable for students with learning difficulties.)
- **World of work** – AEB Basic Tests, Youth Award Scheme
- **Career skills** – GNVQ intermediate level unit (currently being piloted), Edexcel advanced and intermediate Business units, City and Guilds Key Skills 3615 Career Planning Unit

Careers activities can also provide a context for assessed work in GCSE and GNVQ courses. For example:

- GCSE English – talking about work-experience
- GCSE Religious Education – investigating the meaning and nature of work
- GNVQ Foundation level 'Investigating working in ...' units – labour market studies

Various national and local schemes have also been developed to recognise students' achievements, such as the 'Careers Library User's Award' from Birmingham Careers Service, the Project Trident Challenge (work-experience, community service and personal challenge) and the Young Enterprise Certificates (mini enterprise, and team enterprise for students with special needs).

Some schemes allow considerable flexibility so that schools and colleges can assess and accredit students for courses and activities that they have developed. The ASDAN Youth Award Scheme and the Open College Network offer particularly interesting possibilities.

Curriculum Management

Curriculum Management Processes

Effective management of the careers curriculum requires action on four main fronts, as described below.

Auditing

Auditing, or 'taking stock', involves internal and external environmental appraisal. Internal appraisal takes place when someone asks 'What do we do already in the school's careers programme?'. External appraisal happens when the school considers the requirements and recommendations of official bodies such as the Department for Education and Employment, the Qualifications and Curriculum Authority (QCA) or OFSTED; or when the school takes note of developments in the careers programmes in other similar schools. These questions open the door to further enquiries such as 'What else could we be doing?' or 'What could we do differently in the careers programme?'. Auditing is primarily about checking the baseline and identifying needs.

Planning

Preparing to repeat an existing careers activity or to introduce a change needs to be part of a managed process. Effort put into this stage can often prevent problems emerging later. It is useful to distinguish between long term, medium term and short term planning needs. Engaging in planning at all three levels helps to ensure a balance between having a vision of how you would like careers work to develop in your school and dealing with the practical details of specific plans. Careers co-ordinators will certainly find it helpful to have familiarised themselves with some of the general thinking in education on leadership (e.g. Duignan, 1988) and the management of change (e.g. Fullan, 1987).

Implementation

Carrying through agreed plans involves careful management. Communication strategies, for example, may be particularly important for careers activities that are to be delivered through other staff such as tutors. Properly-targeted staff development may also be part of an implementation strategy (see Section Nine).

Evaluation

Examining the value or worth of an activity in the careers programme in a more or less systematic way may lead to greater effectiveness in all other areas of curriculum management. Not everything can be evaluated at once, but it is important to build in manageable and purposeful evaluation activities (see Section Twelve).

The Tools of Curriculum Management

The most useful tools for managing the careers curriculum include those described below.

A careers policy

A policy should represent a school-wide agreement about the nature and purpose of careers education and guidance, and the part that it will play in the overall curriculum. Figure 3.3 (adapted from *Managing Careers Work* (Careers Enterprise Group 1996)) outlines a possible format for a careers policy statement.

Figure 3.3 Suggested format for a careers policy statement.

Heading or section	Commentary
title	Give the policy a title.
intentions of the policy	The school's intention may be to fulfil statutory obligations or to achieve important school aims through careers work. This section may well refer to the unique circumstances and needs of students who attend the school.
how the policy was developed	A policy developed through consultation and agreement has more likelihood of being implemented than one drafted by the careers co-ordinator in isolation.
the school's commitment	A concise statement of what the school believes to be the scope and value of careers work will provide everyone involved in its delivery with a clear understanding and sense of direction.
how the policy will be implemented	This section enables the school to explain: ● staff roles and responsibilities (e.g. the role of the careers co-ordinator) ● partnership arrangements (e.g. working with the local careers service) ● curriculum provision (e.g. timetable arrangements) ● the accommodation that will be made available (e.g. a careers library) ● other resources to be provided (e.g. how staffing levels and capitation will be determined)
how the policy will be evaluated	Arrangements for checking the impact of the careers programme need to be made clear, for example, through an annual review and report.
relationship to other school policies	Careers education and guidance needs both to reflect and contribute to other whole-school policies such as those directed towards equal opportunities, special needs and information technology capability.
signatures	The headteacher and the Chair of Governors may sign the policy.
date	This serves as a reminder of when the policy was formulated.
date of next review	Changing labour markets and education and training systems make it necessary to keep the policy under regular review.

Entitlement statement(s)

Entitlement statements tell students how they can benefit from the school's careers provision. It is important, therefore, that they are written in language that students can easily follow. In terms of curriculum management, schools benefit from developing entitlement statements that clarify the objectives of the careers programme and indicate specific and measurable outcomes for students. Entitlement statements are less effective as a curriculum management tool when they are too modest and insufficiently challenging, and when they promise benefits that students do not particularly value or want. An entitlement statement for a group of students will outline the aims and objectives of the careers provision, the opportunities that will be provided during the year and the expected outcomes, in terms of both enhanced understanding and capability.

A development plan

Senior managers and governors use development planning as a tool for deciding on school goals and the best ways of achieving them. Careers education and guidance, on a par with other subjects and aspects of provision, should be the focus of a development plan. The purpose of a careers education and guidance development plan is two-fold:

1. to show how careers work will contribute to the achievement of some or all of the priorities in the school development plan e.g. if raising achievement is a whole-school priority, the careers development plan should show in practical terms how careers work can be developed to contribute to raising students' achievement
2. to crystallise the other targets and goals for further developing careers work in the school

When constructing a careers education and guidance development plan, it is important to set realistically challenging and costed targets, taking into account, for example, the planning and negotiations involved in reaching a partnership agreement with your local careers service. If you have too many targets, you may undermine the benefits of the process. Development planning should enable you to experience the satisfaction of reaching your goals rather than reinforce the feelings of guilt over unfinished tasks. A useful format for laying out each target in the development plan is suggested in Figure 3.4.

Figure 3.4 Suggested format for a careers education development plan.

Heading or section	Aim
target	to do what?
timescale	by when?
performance indicators	to what standard?
staff	led by whom?
resources	what is needed?

Further advice on development planning can be found in Section Eight.

Audits

When planning an audit, remember to keep it manageable. Limited audits, used sparingly, can be highly effective curriculum management tools. Complex audits are often too time-consuming and difficult for respondents to complete; and the careers co-ordinator may experience problems in analysing, interpreting and following-up the information gained from the audit.

Audits may be tackled in different ways. You may decide to send round a questionnaire, or to interview staff, or to use both approaches. Each has its advantages and disadvantages. Care is needed with the design of questionnaires, for example, to make them unambiguous and user-friendly. Interviews may take up more time, but help to improve communication and build relationships with colleagues who contribute to the careers programme.

Curriculum guidelines

Curriculum guidelines can provide a summary of the careers education and guidance programme in a public document for the benefit of the staff involved in its delivery, and for senior management, other staff, OFSTED and possibly even parents.

Schools have flexibility over the content and format of guidelines, which can be presented in whichever way best suits the school. Typically, guidelines for careers education and guidance will cover the following information:

1. **aims and objectives** of careers education and guidance in the school
2. **key principles** in the design of the careers programme (e.g. differentiation, progression, equal opportunities)
3. **teaching and learning** approaches
4. **assessment and accreditation** of learning
5. **schemes of work** for each year group

Schemes of work

Schools are required to make schemes of work available to parents on request. The benefits of well-produced schemes of work are that they help the teacher to focus on the key career learning targets for specific activities or units of work. They can also help teachers to improve the organisation of learning activities, and provide a record so that teachers do not have to start from scratch the following year. Table 3.8 shows a scheme of work for helping Year 9 students with their Key Stage 4 curricular choices.

Lesson plans

Lesson plans are a vital ingredient of short term planning and are essential where the delivery of part of the programme has been delegated to tutors or other staff by the careers co-ordinator. Schools may have their own preferred format for lesson plans. The format shown in Figure 3.5 can be used or adapted.

Figure 3.5 Suggested format for a careers education lesson plan.

Heading or section	Commentary
year/class	
lesson number	
date	
title/topic	
summary	brief overview of the aim or purpose of the lesson
outcomes	intended learning outcomes
preparation/resources	
differentiation/special needs	
steps	sequence of tasks for teacher and students from introduction through to conclusion, with approximate timings for each step
extension/follow-up	homework; links to other areas of the curriculum; links to next lesson; any evaluation to be undertaken

Table 3.8   Scheme of work for Year 9 students.

Year/group: **9H**   Staff: **AJS**   Term: **Spring**

Aims: **To prepare students for making Key Stage 4 curricular choices**   No. x length of lessons: **5 x 40 minutes**

Lesson No	1	2	3	4	5
Summary	Introduction to choices at 13+. Subjects available at KS4. Qualifications to which they lead (explanation of assessment and awards). Principle of choosing a balanced educational diet.	Begin action-planning and decision-making processes. Choosing an appropriate decision-making strategy. Identifying research questions and incorporating those in an action plan.	Investigate subjects. Assess own needs, interests and strengths in relation to subjects. Review negotiation skills. Consider issue of stereotyping of certain school subjects. Consider how the content and skills developed by subjects are used in adult and working life.	Investigate careers. Find out about subjects that are useful for specific careers, which interest the student now. Identify the next career decision points.	Review action-plans and decision-making strategies. Complete record of current thinking for careers portfolio. Reminder of timetable of remaining events. Identify outstanding difficulties and action to be taken.
Intended outcomes	Commitment and involvement of students in relation to making choices.	Ability to select a decision-making strategy which is 'fit for purpose'. Ability to initiate and draw up a simple action plan following a given format.	Awareness of subjects as a way of organising the learning of useful content and skills. Ability to recognise and challenge stereotyping of school subjects.	Awareness of entry requirements for careers which are currently of interest to the student.	Understanding of need for self-reliance and self-motivation in career planning.
Preparation and resources	Which Way Now booklet. School options booklet. Handout on 'design your ideal timetable'.	Decision-making handout. Action-planning proforma. Who Me? Video	Access to careers library. Handout on negotiation skills.	Access to careers library.	Record sheet for careers portfolio.
Teaching and Learning methods	Whole-class instruction and question-and-answer session.	Individual and paired work.	Individual and paired work.	Individual and paired work.	Individual and paired work.
Assessment and homework	HW – Read booklets.	HW – Carry out tasks in action plan			Keep completed record sheet in careers portfolio/profile.
Other curriculum links	Parents' information evening.	Meet some of last year's Y9 students in tutor group meeting to discuss how they made their choices.	Talks in assemblies by Heads of Departments		

Evaluation reports

The evaluation of aspects of the careers programme is dealt with in Section Twelve. Planned evaluation reports help curriculum management by drawing to the attention of school decision-makers those areas of the careers programme that are working well and those that could be developed further.

An annual report to senior managers and governors can provide a useful summary of achievements. The report might include:

- analysis of the destinations of leavers
- careers co-ordinator's report on the year's main achievements
- report on the work experience scheme
- statistical analysis of the main work accomplished by careers staff, including the link careers adviser (e.g. number of interviews)

Action Points

☐ Identify the learning outcomes that you expect students to achieve at each Key Stage and 16–19.

☐ Work out how the possible interactions shown in the model of the learning process (Figure 3.1) can be managed to maximise students' learning gains.

☐ Audit your use of different teaching and learning methods in the careers programme based on Table 3.3 and the activity that follows.

☐ Clarify your approach to assessment in careers education and guidance and check that it is consistent with the school's overall policy on assessment.

☐ Review the possibilities for accrediting students' learning in careers education and guidance.

☐ Review your approach to curriculum planning and development in careers education and guidance.

Section Four

Careers Guidance

In Section Four we learn that:

☛ *Schools and careers services each need to understand the other's contribution to the guidance process. A code of practice can help to achieve this understanding.*

☛ *Teachers and tutors often provide students with careers-related guidance, albeit unwittingly. The careers co-ordinator must be clear about what role he/she wishes other teachers to play in relation to guidance, and to ensure that staff development is available to support them in this work.*

☛ *Agreeing a set of principles for your guidance work with students will help to secure good standards of practice.*

☛ *Students need to be prepared for guidance.*

☛ *Teachers providing guidance will benefit from using a model of practice upon which to base their interviews.*

☛ *Key counselling skills, such as 'active listening', are important for interviewers.*

☛ *Preparing for interviews should involve four basic considerations:*
  1. *what resources and materials the interviewer needs for the interview*
  2. *what the interviewee needs to be told – the location, time, probable duration, and what to bring*
  3. *a basic plan for the interview including aims and objectives*
  4. *a suitable venue for the interview*

☛ *Action-planning should be fitted into a broader perspective of careers-related guidance.*

☛ *Small-group work can offer a valuable context for careers-related guidance.*

This Section looks at why students need careers guidance and considers how this need can be met by teachers and tutors. The Section also examines the key components of guidance-related activities and some of the possible methods that can be used to support students' career learning and development.

Clarity about Roles

The School and Careers Service

Guidance is an area of careers work in which consensus about roles and responsibilities is sometimes hard to achieve both within the school, and between the school and the careers service. Some of the reasons for this are discussed later (see Section Ten). Clarification and agreement about the respective roles and responsibilities of the school and the careers service is really quite fundamental to securing effective complementary practice.

Schools clearly have a major responsibility in providing students with educational guidance, and careers services have a statutory responsibility to provide students with careers guidance. In practice, the distinction between educational guidance and careers guidance is very hard to maintain, since invariably each 'agency' will intrude into the other's territory. Although such intrusions are often for entirely legitimate reasons, schools and careers services sometimes foster a degree of suspicion about each other's motives and intentions as far as careers guidance is concerned.

Nervousness about post 16 retention makes some schools reluctant to offer information and advice on post 16 options at other institutions. The same concern can make schools anxious about the activities of careers services, which aim to provide independent advice to all students.

In order to ensure that the careers guidance students experience is as helpful as it can be, it is a good idea for the school and the careers service to agree a code of practice clarifying their complementary roles.

> Is there scope in your school for setting in place a code of practice between the school and the careers service, agreeing what guidance each institution will provide? For example, can the school agree to provide guidance on educational options offered internally but allow the careers service to provide detailed information and guidance on the range of opportunities elsewhere?

Teachers and Tutors

Although careers guidance sometimes appears to be a 'bolt on' activity, in reality a lot of careers-related guidance takes place during the daily transactions between tutors and their students. The key issue here is whether tutors are alert to this or not, and whether they know what is expected of them and what contribution they are able to make.

> What roles do you expect tutors to play in careers-related guidance? Do you expect them to:
> - occasionally supplement existing guidance work?
> - regularly use tutorial time to support or underpin existing guidance work?
> - have responsibility for delivering key components of guidance work?

Some tutors 'shy away' from careers-related guidance because of their concerns about giving wrong information. However, just as all teachers should be able to advise students about generic study skills, irrespective of their area(s) of expertise, it can be argued that all teachers should be able to help their students with basic career research tasks. They can do this by encouraging students to develop and apply skills such as planning, information processing, decision-making, and so on. Teachers and tutors can provide effective and varied support without having to be 'careers experts' but they may need some staff development to help them understand their own skills and how these can be best utilised (see Table 4.1).

Table 4.1   **Core skills used by tutors in guidance activities (from _Choice for the Future_, Book 6 (1991) prepared for TVEI by 'Learners First').**

These core skills are, in the main, interpersonal skills that many of us use in an unconscious way in our everyday lives; a number of teachers and lecturers are conscious of the importance of these skills and have a significant degree of insight into them. This is not, however, the case with all adults who have an influence over the career development of 16 to 19-year-olds. The task of improving and co-ordinating provision implies helping some people to acquire new skills and others to refine existing ones.	
Listening	a core skill that involves concentrating fully on what the student says and using silence constructively
Non-verbal communication	paying attention to, and making use of, non-verbal behaviour to gain a fuller understanding of what the student is saying
Questioning	using questions to clarify what the student is saying and to encourage him/her to say more. This involves the appropriate use of both open and closed questions
Feeding back	reflecting back what the student is saying. This can, in some situations, involve offering interpretation of what the student is saying
Confronting	helping the student to become more self-aware by highlighting apparent inconsistencies in what he/she says or by helping him/her to see the consequences of his/her actions. This must be done sensitively and appropriately

The quality of guidance that tutors provide does vary (Whiteside, 1994). Tutorials can provide an excellent context for supporting students in guidance-related enquiries (Edwards, 1995), but tutors still need to know what they can legitimately do. Is their brief:

- to provide 'first aid' guidance in a crisis?
- to provide 'front-line' guidance and support?
- to help students to plan and review career learning?
- to know how and when to refer to others with particular careers expertise?

Perhaps the tutors' brief should involve all of these activities, some of which will require the use of the core skills referred to in Table 4.1. Teachers and tutors should be trained to acquire and practise some of these guidance skills.

A decision must be made about the role that tutors are expected to play in careers guidance.

- Who is responsible for making this decision?
- Has the decision been explained and is it being properly implemented and monitored?
- Are there staff development needs that ought to be addressed to help tutors in this role?

Key Elements of the Guidance Process

Students receive guidance from a range of sources, not just from the school. The influence of the home has been well documented over recent years; so too has the influence of the peer group and 'significant others' from the community. Guidance can be solicited or unsolicited; formal or informal; from adults or peers; and independent or partial. Students will make decisions about the guidance that they receive based upon their own value systems, and their views of themselves and of the world. Their gender, ethnicity, life history and physical disposition will all affect their evaluation of the guidance they receive, and the decisions they subsequently make.

Principles for Guidance

Guidance provided in school is not the only source of help available to students, but it is – or should be – different in a number of respects to guidance provided elsewhere and by other people. Guidance from school should:

- be 'student-centred', primarily concerned with the needs of the student, above the needs of the organisation or system
- be managed as a professional and ethical activity, requiring objective, impartial and accessible information and guidance
- have educational value in that it helps students to understand the skills associated with planning, researching, negotiating, reflecting, and making and implementing choices, so that they are able to use these processes more independently for themselves
- help students to make their own voice heard, to be able to 'tell their own story' and to have this valued and respected
- help students to make 'connections' between their 'different lives' and identities, lived out in school, at home and in the community
- help students to make reasoned assessments of what they can know about themselves, their achievements, their potential and the opportunities that may be open to them

What do students need to understand about guidance?

In a review of guidance-related research, Killeen and Kidd (1992) stressed the importance of students' 'readiness for guidance'. Students need to know and understand:

- what guidance means, and what it involves
- when guidance will be available during their school careers
- how one-to-one or small-group guidance operates
- what real benefits can be gained from the conversations they will have with teaching staff and careers advisers

Students will also need to appreciate who else can offer guidance, and recognise how to discriminate between objective and balanced guidance and that which is biased or simply misleading. We can mistakenly assume that students already know the purpose, function and value of guidance, when in fact many do not. It is all the more important, therefore, for careers-related guidance to be presented as a non-threatening activity, which is primarily concerned with students needs and interests.

How and when do you introduce your students to the guidance dimension of careers work?

Is guidance explained in adequate detail, and presented in an inviting and non-threatening manner?

How could your existing practice be changed for the better?

What does the careers co-ordinator need to know about guidance?

The principles for guidance listed above are fairly consistent with 'person-centred' approaches to guidance and counselling. Ali and Graham (1996, pages 44–61) have produced a person-centred model for interviewing based upon the earlier work in Gerard Egan's *Skilled Helper* and Sue Culley's *Integrative Counselling Skills in Action*. Ali and Graham (ibid.) argue that interviews conducted with students can be improved by following a model of practice (see Table 4.2). They describe the model as:

...the foundation of the careers interview, which provides a firm structure designed to achieve the desired outcome, namely that the student has moved on in some way along the process of career planning. Without this firm base, the interview will resemble a cosy chat...

Table 4.2 Model of practice for conducting careers guidance interviews (after Ali and Graham).

1. Clarifying phase	<ul><li>setting the scene</li><li>developing empathy</li><li>hearing the student's story</li><li>making an initial assessment</li></ul>
2. Exploring phase	<ul><li>building the contract</li><li>exploring the issues within the contract</li><li>encouraging the student to explore other options</li><li>re-examining the contract</li></ul>
3. Evaluating phase	<ul><li>challenging inconsistencies</li><li>prioritising options with the student</li><li>re-examining the contract</li></ul>
4. Action-planning phase	<ul><li>helping the student to identify what needs to be done</li><li>encouraging the student to form a plan of action</li><li>introducing the concept of referral, if necessary</li><li>ending the interview</li></ul>

The framework outlined in Table 4.2 suggests the sort of phases through which a guidance interview should ideally proceed. Some of these phases will be completed more speedily than others. In some instances, further meetings might be required to work through all parts of the process. It is a model of guidance for the interviewer and not a straightjacket that dictates how every single interview should be conducted. This type of model lends itself quite well to the development of practice and self-assessment.

> Try using the framework in Table 4.2 as a basis for conducting your own guidance interviews. If you are unfamiliar with this type of process, it might take a little time to become comfortable with the four stages described, but once you have 'internalised' them you will find that you have a means of developing effective 'guidance conversations'.

Effective interviews also rest upon the application of basic counselling skills, some of which are briefly described in Table 4.1. Active listening, especially, is one of the key skills central to guidance practice. Rogers and Farson (1976) offer the following description:

> *The kind of listening we have in mind is called 'active listening'. It is called 'active' because the listener has a very definite responsibility. He does not passively absorb the words that are spoken to him. He actively tries to grasp the facts and feelings in what he hears, and he tries, by his listening, to help the speaker work out his own problems.*

Rogers and Farson (ibid.) also claim that active listening is an important means of bringing about changes in people:

> *When people are listened to sensitively, they tend to listen to themselves with more care and make clear exactly what they are feeling and thinking.*

Although this approach to 'listening' has it roots in a therapeutic and counselling context, active listening remains an important technique within careers guidance. It is the basis upon which we can build and utilise many of the other key skills such as summarising, reflecting back, paraphrasing, questioning, and so on.

I know you believe you understand what you think I said, but I am not sure you realise that what you heard is not what I meant.

Preparing to Conduct an Interview

The best interviews are those for which you have had time to prepare. Assuming that you are clear about the overall purpose of the interview, and that this has been shared and agreed with the student beforehand, four basic considerations need to be remembered.

1. **What do you need for the interview?**
    You might need to take resources and documents to the interview, such as essential paperwork, forms, files, portfolios, records, letters, reference books, a computer etc.

2. **What does the interviewee need?**
    The reason or purpose for the interview will depend upon the needs of the interviewee. Explain and agree the purpose beforehand, in order to help avoid the anxiety that some students harbour in advance of an interview. Students need to know when and where to come, how long the interview might take and whether they need to bring anything with them. Ideally, students should not be kept waiting, but where this is unavoidable, at least try to arrange somewhere comfortable for the interviewee to wait and keep him/her informed. Nobody wants to be kept hanging around wondering what is going on.

3. **What should the interview include?**
    It is best to have a basic plan for the interview, which includes your aims and objectives. The interview model referred to in Table 4.2 provides a route through the interview, as well as suggesting what you should look for on the way.

    In beginning any interview, you should pay attention to building rapport and establishing empathy with the student. You should also agree what will be discussed and the time available (making the contract) before entering into the early exploratory phase of the interview. Be systematic and avoid leaping from one topic to another. Make notes if it helps, but agree this with the student first.

You will find that some things are quite factual and therefore relatively easy to check, whereas other points – such as attitude, feelings, motive, and intention – are less easy to determine. Sometimes an interview is like a piece of detective work where you (or the student) may hold certain hypotheses that need to be tested. You will be gathering information and sharing information too. The student may want to gather some information of his/her own. This possible eventuality requires some prior thought:

- What information might the student require?
- What is the student entitled to know?
- At what point in the interview should information be disclosed or shared?
- How should you deal with sensitive information?

These are just some examples of the types of issues for which you may have to prepare in your interview plan.

4. **Where should the interview be conducted?**
The ideal physical setting for an interview is not always available, given the usual constraints on space in school. However, the physical layout of the room should be considered carefully, as it can influence the success of the interview. Below are listed some factors that can have adverse affects on the outcome:

- sitting behind a desk (implies formality and can therefore be a barrier)
- seating the interviewee on a lower chair than yourself
- looking at the interviewee across a desk filled with clutter
- sitting at a distance from the interviewee
- sitting too close to the interviewee
- placing the interviewee in an uncomfortable position – in direct sunlight, or close to a doorway, for example
- being subject to interruptions

Sorry to have kept you waiting...
Now, where did I put your file...

These are just some of the ways in which rapport can be undermined – all of which can be avoided easily by routine preparation. The key point is that the physical setting can affect the ease of communication.

Careers-Related Guidance and Action-Planning

Young people need to plan for their futures. This is not a contentious point. Various sources of recent research have stressed the need for individuals to accept more responsibility for managing their own careers, given that conventional notions of 'career' are increasingly seen as outmoded in the labour market of the late 1990s. The process of action-planning has important value in this respect. It provides a useful method for self-exploration, and for recording written data about one's present situation and the steps that need to be taken in pursuit of individual goals. Much has been written about the potential benefits and problems of action-planning, and readers who wish to examine the subject in more detail should follow up the references in the bibliography.

What Does Action-Planning Mean?

A precise definition of action-planning, which covers every context in which some form of the process is used, is difficult to formulate. Squirrel (1995), however, has suggested that the cycle of individual action-planning should engage students in:

- raising self-awareness
- considering their broad aspirations
- identifying their development needs
- collecting relevant information and discussing their aspirations, learning needs and education or training options with an impartial counsellor
- planning broad goals
- setting smaller actionable targets, which are time-bound and accompanied by success criteria to facilitate monitoring
- reviewing actions and experiences and re-formulating targets, timescales or even broad goals if necessary

The concept and practice of individual action-planning have diversified in recent years, both in terms of the ages of students with whom they are used and in the scope and purpose of their application. While this may have led generally to rich and diverse forms of practice, it has also created a degree of confusion in its wake. Watts (1991, pages 6–7) has attempted to unravel some of the tangle by distinguishing four primary views of action-planning.

1. The first view is that action-planning is a **pupil-management** process, aiming to involve pupils in taking more responsibility for their own behaviour and learning **within the school.**

2. The second view is that action-planning is a **guidance** process, aiming to help individuals to set targets at key **transition points.**

3. The third view is that action-planning is an **educational** process, aiming to help individuals to develop lifeskills that will be of value to them on a lifetime basis.

4. The fourth view is that all three previous elements can be brought together by seeing action-planning as a **management of learning** process, aiming to encourage individuals to take more responsibility for the direction of their own learning on a continuing basis.

Use the following questions to carry out an initial audit of action-planning practice within your school.

1. Who is using action-planning in your school or college?

2. What is their primary purpose, and with which groups of students is the process being used?

3. Is there any form of 'dialogue' between users so that practice is harmonised and co-ordinated?

4. How well do Squirell's seven 'principles' compare with existing practice?

5. Are students' experiences monitored and evaluated? Are these findings fed back into the system?

You may discover that the practice of action-planning in your school is less well co-ordinated than you had expected. It is also possible that you will encounter different points of view in relation to the **process** and **product** of action-planning, i.e. whether the primary aim is the guidance process and dialogue between the teacher/careers adviser and student, or the actual product or document, which may be for private use by the student or for accountability purposes (for performance-related funding).

Action-Planning Within the Context of Careers Guidance

Recent research suggests that there is now broad agreement about the purpose of the action-planning process, in promoting students' planning and review skills, for example. However, important differences remain about the role of the product and whether it should feature as a private or public document. Moreover, this tension between the 'process' and 'product' of action-planning impinges upon the role of the careers service in careers guidance and upon its capacity to meet demanding output-related targets. There is always a risk that the requirement by the system for a product will begin to override the action-planning process.

There is also the risk that tutors and students will begin to regard action-planning as synonymous with guidance. Action-planning needs to be seen as part of the careers guidance process and not the other way around. Action-planning is a valuable technique or device to assist in the latter stages of the careers guidance process when individuals are ready and able to identify research and implementation strategies (which may be very simple) that can benefit from a linear and chronological presentation. The argument here, however, is that any such device should be subservient to the overarching process of guidance, which must have broader concerns about facilitating ongoing dialogue and exploration, rather than upon an exclusive concern for decision-making.

Decisions, in any event, hinge upon so many other factors, which need to be worked through. Self-exploration has already been mentioned. To this we can add the processes of reconciling and dealing with competing demands and pressures which arise from each student's unique lifestyle and experiences. Students need, too, to be able to base their decision-making upon a workable conceptual framework which will enable them to understand enough of how the educational and occupational systems operate and how the opportunities available to them can be accessed and managed. It is not that decision-making is unimportant, but rather that if most of the effort being invested in careers guidance is focused upon the latter stages of the process, there is always the risk that important personal issues will have gone unnoticed or remain unresolved.

A further danger of an instrumental view of the action-planning procedure, is that students can be left with an incorrect impression that they have somehow reached the end of the decision-making process and that guidance has no further value. This model has some similarities with the prescription process used by general practitioners. If the medicine fails to do the job, the onus is upon the patient to return for further advice. Of course, in this scenario, not everyone bothers, even though they may need to. For this reason, guidance in a school context should function not only as an individual activity, but also as part of the pastoral or tutorial system. This means that students should be followed up and encouraged to review their progress and, where appropriate, to re-consider goals or devise alternative strategies, thereby helping them to forge a deeper level of commitment to their decision-making. Learning frequently takes us through cyclical or 'spiral-like' stages of enquiry, experience and reflection. Guidance practice likewise needs to take into account the fact that career learning is neither linear nor an automatic and progressive outcome of action-planning per se.

Is the process-versus-product dichotomy one that you have already encountered?

What issues has it raised for staff and students involved in careers guidance?

Have you found workable strategies for reaching common understanding and agreement?

Does scope exist for students to have individual or group guidance before their interview with the careers adviser?

Case Study

The careers co-ordinator and careers adviser recognised the importance of the Year 11 careers guidance interviews, and wanted to ensure that each student was as fully prepared as possible. However, there was much anecdotal evidence to suggest that many students were ill-prepared to consider and discuss some of the basic but important questions raised by the careers adviser during these interviews. The careers co-ordinator raised this concern with her SMT, and was invited to consider potential ways of improving the situation, which did not demand any additional curriculum time, but which made better use of existing tutorial periods.

After some consideration, it was felt that form tutors should be asked to support the assessment of students' career learning during Years 9 and 10 so that the two careers specialists could monitor the progression and development of each individual's ideas, and take action as appropriate. This meant revising the 'career learning' opportunities within the curriculum, and using the careers adviser's time more flexibly during lunch periods so that individual students could have informal contact with him on an ongoing basis during Years 9 and 10.

The careers co-ordinator and careers adviser reviewed the desired learning outcomes for each of the four careers education modules, which were delivered through PSHE during Years 9 and 10. They reconstructed these learning outcomes into two sets of profile statements: one set for each form tutor, and another, in easier language, for use by the students. The intention was to make it more explicit to the students exactly what they should learn at each stage of the careers programme and to involve them in a process of self-assessment. Form tutors were provided with a profile sheet for each student.

Assessments were completed by the students at the end of each careers module. Over a three week period, form tutors discussed and reviewed each student's own assessment of his/her learning and completed a profile indicating areas of development and need. These profile sheets were returned to the careers co-ordinator so that she could assess the impact of the careers modules, and identify areas of unmet need for future curriculum planning and individual guidance.

This system of monitoring and assessment involved students in the use of planning and reviewing skills much earlier than was previously the case, although no reference to action-planning was made at this stage. It also ensured that individual students were given more time and opportunity to develop the career knowledge and skills that they would ultimately need to apply later in their school lives.

Do you use a system of monitoring and assessment of career learning like that in the case study in your school at the moment?

How could you use or adapt the case study example to improve your own practice?

Guidance Work with Groups

Careers education and guidance already occurs in groups, in the sense that a class or a tutorial group will undertake activities together as part of the curriculum programme. An important question for guidance purposes, however, is how such groups can become an additional and effective context for work of this sort. Group work can be threatening to some and quite liberating to others. It can offer an important opportunity to 'hear one's own voice' and also to hear the 'voices' of others, recounting their own hopes, fears and learning experiences. Stanford and Stoate (1991) offer both practical and informed strategies for creating and nurturing effective groups, which while relevant to learning in general, also include insights especially useful for guidance work. They have identified five stages involved in developing effective classroom groups.

Stage One: Orientation (forming)

Questions students ask	Helpful teacher behaviour
What is going to happen here? What will the experience be like?	Explain what students can expect in your class or tutor group.
Who are the other people here? What are they like?	Help students to get acquainted with you and with one another.
Where do I fit in with these people? How will I be treated here?	Be a model of the behaviour you expect.

'Getting acquainted' and trust-building exercises are essential to this stage – they help to set the ground rules for the group's work and enable students to share information and seek common ideas.

Stage Two: Establishing Norms (norming)

During this stage you should help the students to develop new skills and attitudes in order for the group to move on to maturity.

1. **Group responsibility** – leadership emerges from the group itself; everybody contributes to the work of the group.

2. **Responsiveness to others** – members listen in depth to one another and link together their ideas to build a group product.

3. **Interdependence** – members co-operate to achieve goals rather than competing with one another.

4. **Decision-making through consensus** – the group arrives at decisions satisfactory to all, rather than imposing the will of the majority on the minority.

5. **Confronting problems** – disagreements are faced instead of being ignored, and solutions are sought.

The key point at this stage is to give the group as much responsibility as you can.

Stage Three: Coping with Conflict (storming)

Stanford believes that if a group remains together, and the leader (tutor) continues to give attention to group dynamics and helps the group to move ahead, then a period of conflict predictably arises, although the reasons for this are not completely clear. He suggests five characteristics of helpful teacher behaviour in the conflict stage.

1. Explain that conflict can be a positive force.

2. Provide support and reassurance for students who feel anxious about open expression of conflict.

3. Don't become more authoritarian.

4. Utilise active listening.

5. Respond to the feelings underlying the students' words.

Structured approaches for resolving conflicts are offered in Table 4.3 (overleaf).

Table 4.3   Approaches for resolving conflicts.

Using 'I' messages	An 'I' message is a statement of how a person's actions make you feel. It gives information about the impact a person is having on you, whereas a 'You' message can be interpreted as an attempt to label or blame someone.
Negotiating no-lose situations	The objective is to find solutions to which both parties are willing to commit themselves.
The four-step strategy	● utilise active listening ● convey understanding and acceptance ● describe your own feelings using an 'I' message ● negotiate a no-lose solution
Role reversal	Ask two people in conflict to spend a few minutes trying to 'think' themselves into the other person's situation.
You say/I say	Each person summarises the point that the other was making, to the satisfaction of the other person.
The 3R strategy	Encourage each person to: ● work through **R**esentment ● request specific actions from the other person that will **R**educe conflict ● **R**ecognise which of the other person's requests they would be prepared to meet
Third-party mediation	Facilitate agreement with the help of a mediator.

Stage Four: Productivity (performing)

This is the point at which the group has become a mature working unit and possesses the skills and attitudes necessary for effective interaction in learning activities. Students should be able to work together to accomplish a variety of learning tasks and can deal with disagreement and interpersonal conflict in constructive ways. However, you will need to help the group to maintain its skills and to be prepared for temporary regression.

Stage Five: Termination (mourning)

Stanford acknowledges that groups that have developed through stages one to four are likely to experience a 'rather stormy termination stage'. But 'mourning' also provides an opportunity to celebrate individually and collectively what the group has achieved (Table 4.4).

Effective Careers Education and Guidance

Table 4.4 Characteristics of the termination stage, and associated helpful teacher behaviour.

Characteristics	Helpful teacher behaviour
● increased conflict ● breakdown of group skills ● lethargy ● frantic attempts to work well ● anger at the teacher ● tie up any loose ends	● acknowledge that the group is really ending ● encourage students to express their feelings related to termination ● help students to review the experience ● help the group to work out a way to immortalise the experience ● explore ways students can begin to reinvest their emotional energy

A key point here is to remember that endings are also beginnings.

An effective group can provide an excellent forum for dealing with and managing guidance-related issues. These may be class groups, smaller tutor groups, or groups of students who come together to explore or discuss a particular topic, perhaps at lunch times or after school. The emphasis should be not so much on using the group as a means of conveying information, but on helping students to gain new insights and self-knowledge, and to practise communication and inter-personal skills that will increase their own maturity and understanding. It can also be reassuring for students to learn that the challenges, pressures and anxieties sometimes associated with career choice are shared by their peers.

The topics best suited to the group approach are therefore those that focus upon issues, challenges, needs and concerns. Some examples of such topics are listed below:

- knowing more about myself
- making decisions about the future
- leaving home and going to college
- dealing with prejudice about disabilities
- de-briefing after work-experience – reviewing what I have learned and relating it to my future choices
- preparing for different kinds of interviews
- getting a job – how can I improve my prospects?

The group learning approach is one that could also involve the careers adviser, either as the group facilitator, or as a resource to the group.

Having reviewed the school's annual student destination statistics, a careers co-ordinator was increasingly concerned at the narrow range of career areas to which the majority of female students were aspiring. Although issues such as sexual discrimination and gender stereotyping had been covered in the PSHE programme, there seemed to be no change in girls' inclinations to enter typically 'female occupations', even when the spread of ability suggested that far more ambitious and wide-ranging careers were achievable.

The co-ordinator wanted to learn more about the reasons that limited the girls' career choices, while also trying new ways of 'exposing' them to alternative perspectives and ideas. To help with this she enlisted the support of the local Education–Business Partnership to find two women from the local business community who had successfully established themselves in traditional male occupations. These visitors were to provide a reference point for the discussion although the careers co-ordinator would retain the role of group facilitator.

The co-ordinator announced in a Year 10 assembly that she wanted to invite a pilot group of 15 girls to three lunchtime meetings, which would be spread over a half-term period. The purpose of the group was explained and interested girls were invited to a 10 minute briefing session that lunchtime. During the meeting the girls were given a handout explaining what the meetings were for, what was going to happen, who would be there and how the group would operate. The careers co-ordinator also explained the ground rules to the group about respect for different points of view, etc. Finally, she asked each of the girls to complete a questionnaire on the type of work-experience placement they were hoping for in the coming summer term.

Most girls attended all three sessions bringing a packed lunch with them. The careers co-ordinator provided soft drinks and tea and coffee. Each session lasted 40 minutes, although once discussion got going, they could have run on much longer. The discussion generated a lot of ideas and strong feelings. During the second session, some sensitive issues came to the fore but the group showed its ability to live and learn through some high and low points in the discussion. The 'witness' and perspective of the visitor was invaluable in helping students to ask real and searching questions about real life situations and how they could be handled.

Do you use a group learning approach already?

Could you use such an approach as part of the careers-related guidance work in your school? How could you make it happen?

What topics in your careers guidance programme could be addressed using this approach?

Who would need to be involved and how could they be supported?

Action Points

☐ Agree a code of practice with the careers service.

☐ Decide on the role that tutors should play in your careers guidance programme. Ensure that the decision is explained, implemented and monitored. Provide staff development as required.

☐ Ensure that your students understand the purpose, function and value of guidance.

☐ Assess your current guidance practice against the principles for guidance listed. Decide how improvements could be made.

☐ Review the use made of action-planning by colleagues in your school. Decide how practice can be developed to ensure guidance opportunities for students are optimised.

☐ Evaluate your students' perspectives on your current guidance programme. Decide how improvements could be made.

☐ Plan and prepare for a careers interview using the model and guidelines provided.

☐ Consider how group work is used in your current guidance programme. Decide how it could be extended and improved.

Section Five

Working with Information

> **In Section Five we learn that:**
>
> ☛ **Providing students with a range of opportunities to learn and practise information processing skills is of central importance in career learning.**
>
> ☛ **Students will need to use and apply information processing techniques throughout their adult lives, as they attempt to anticipate and respond to the changes in the labour economy that impact upon themselves and their families.**
>
> ☛ **In order to learn, practise and use information processing skills, students need access to high quality careers resources.**

Careers information – or, perhaps more accurately, information about learning and work – is an integral part of any careers provision. Good practice in careers work means that schools and colleges should provide all students with access to a comprehensive range of up-to-date information. During the 1990s, several White Paper initiatives have provided additional funds to schools to ensure a good standard of provision in this respect. Moreover, there is no shortage of helpful published material to assist teachers in setting up and maintaining an effective careers library.

Given the most recent developments in information technology, especially following the introduction of CD-ROMs and the Internet in schools, the scope for accessing information is almost unlimited. The careers libraries that we know today might possibly be unrecognisable in five years time. In a burgeoning information society such as our own, ensuring that students have access to high grade information may therefore become progressively less of an issue for the careers co-ordinator. However, teaching students how to process the information and use it effectively will continue to be vital. It is this second issue which is the prime focus of this Section.

Why Information is Important

Irrespective of how few or many choices are open to a student, decisions about learning and work need to be made on the basis of the best information available. Fredrickson's (1982, page 1) reasoning still retains some currency:

> *Career planning is critical for both the individual and society. It is critical for the individual because it determines so much about the life he or she will live. It is critical for a democratic society because the survival of that society depends upon each member using his or her talents in the most productive and satisfying way to meet the needs of society. Unfortunately, however, the choice of vocation is often left to chance or made with inadequate information.*

The decisions you make about the information you provide can open up or close down the opportunities available to your students (Law, 1991, 1995). This has implications not just for the range but also for the quality of information made available to students. Summerson (1992, pages 15–24) argues that for inclusion within a careers library, information should meet standards of:

- accuracy
- credibility, attractiveness and readability
- language level
- comprehensiveness
- freedom from bias

In Summerson's view, accuracy is the single most important criterion:

> *Inaccurate information is always misleading; at worst, it is downright dangerous and may lead people to take the wrong decisions. In the careers world, information changes very rapidly – especially 'hard' information relating to the facts and figures of the employment scene.*

Auditing a careers library should be an annual task, demanding 'surgical' decisions about what can be retained and what needs to removed. Ongoing monitoring of incoming information also needs to be undertaken. Better still, students could cast a 'critical eye' over the types of careers information they will encounter in your library, and this could constitute one or more activities linked to the development of the information processing skills referred to later.

The careers information you provide must be properly organised. The Careers Library Classification Index (CLCI) is perhaps the most comprehensive and widely used system, but it requires regular and conscientious maintenance. Information should come from a wide variety of sources and be presented using the full range of media, such as print-based, audio-visual and IT-based. The typology in Table 5.1 describes the types of information that a library or resource base should include.

Table 5.1 Types of information that should be included in a careers library.

Labour market data	Occupational information
● information on employers and training providers ● employment trends ● 'manpower' forecasts ● recruitment advertising	● occupational literature showing education and training requirements ● information from professional bodies, training organisations
Educational information	**Lifestyle information**
● course compendia ● prospectuses ● course databases	● job case studies on individuals at work ● interviews with working people (biographical data) ● work-experience reports
Self-help information	**Evaluation and destination data**
● self-study guides ● learning resource materials for self-assessment and planning purposes ● computer assisted learning activities	● attitude questionnaires and surveys ● destinations data

Adapted from Ben Ball (1984) **'Careers Information: A Typology'**

The Importance of Information Processing Skills

That careers libraries need to be managed and properly maintained is beyond dispute. It is an important task and one not to be undervalued. However, the provision of information does not by itself guarantee that students will be either inclined or able to use it for the purposes of their own planning and decision making. Professor Norton Grubb (1996) has used the term 'Information Dump' to describe the volume of information which students may collect for and about themselves during their school career, but asks under what conditions is this information sufficient for decision-making about learning and work. He cites an example from the USA, where the impact of information intended to reduce drug usage or teenage pregnancies is at best uncertain. Young people attribute different types of authority to information. In order to make effective use of information, a high degree of literacy is also required, which can mean that students without this 'skill' are excluded from using the range of information typically on offer. Grubb argues that despite being surrounded by information, students only make use of it if they need to, and do so by forming their own set constructs in order to make meaningful sense of it. How students form constructs about such information remains an important question for further investigation.

Grubb therefore stresses the need for students to have 'facilitative' experiences that will enable them to develop the capacities necessary for information usage. A related view has been taken by Law (1996), who has proposed a theory of career learning that emphasises the importance of understanding in informing action, in a progression of learning sequences connected to work, role and self. Law sees these sequences as incremental, building upon earlier learning, as shown in Table 5.2.

Table 5.2 Progression of learning sequences involved in career learning (after Law).

	Involves students in ...
SENSING ↓	... **gathering information** about what happens in work, role and self ... **assembling information** into meaningful sequences
SIFTING ↓	... **making comparisons** between this and that, now and then, theirs and mine ... **using concepts** using classifying categories
FOCUSING ↓	... **accommodating points-of-view**, seeing things in other ways ... **developing and testing a view**, developing an 'inner life'
UNDERSTANDING ↓	... **developing explanations**, knowing 'why it is like this ...' ... **anticipating consequences**, knowing 'what would happen if ...'
ACTION	

Another view of career learning that requires effective information processing skills is taken from the *Career Choice Education* programme, which has been taught for some years in schools in Quebec and some regions of France. This programme, first developed by researchers Pelletier, Noiseux and Bujold during the early 1980s, describes a series of developmental learning experiences structured around the four principal stages, as shown in Figure 5.1.

In the model of career learning outlined in Figure 5.1, satisfactory progression into activities associated with the third and fourth stages (specifying and implementing) depends upon the student's ability to conceptualise and classify information effectively. The crystallising stage bears some resemblance to Law's 'sifting' sequence (Table 5.2) and begins to suggest a much more important role for information processing skills than is usually assumed in most careers education programmes.

What implications do Law's hypotheses (Table 5.2) and the Canadian scheme (Figure 5.1) have for the ways in which you help students to use and develop information processing skills within your careers programme?

For example, the careers library can never be the *sole* source or repository for the information students need about work, self and role. It provides important access to *some* types of information, which can figure within a learning programme, but strategies are needed to help students locate, process and evaluate different fragments of 'internal' and 'external' information, which they need to use in planning and decision-making.

Figure 5.1   A development approach to careers education.

Tasks in the decision-making process:

- exploring
- crystallising
- specifying
- implementing

Exploring (creative thinking)		Crystallising (conceptual thinking)	
Action verbs	Attitudes	Action verbs	Attitudes
to observe	openness	to reduce	interest
to question	awareness	to relate	self-appraisal
to describe	curiosity	to group	organisation **
to identify	tolerance	to classify	order**
to define	hypothesise	to sum up	continuity **
to imagine ...	imagination	to categorise ...	coherence *

Modes of thought:

- creative thinking
- conceptual thinking
- critical thinking
- relational thinking

Specifying (critical thinking)		Implementing (relational thinking)	
Action verbs	Attitudes	Action verbs	Attitudes
to compare	judgement	to deduce	certainty
to examine	confidence	to anticipate	involvement
to prioritise	responsibility	to apply	efficiency
to eliminate	discrimination	to generalise	insight
to evaluate	critical sense*	to plan	practicality*
to select ...	reflectiveness	to develop ...	determination

*Understood as sense of ...

** Understood as preference for ...

'Relational thinking' refers to the processes that generate information in a logical, practical and sequential way.

(Taken from **'Careers Choice Education - Curriculum Guide'** *Ministry of Education, Quebec 1991.)*

Developing Strategies for Students' Learning

Information processing skills are, of course, not the concern of careers co-ordinators alone. Students need the capability to locate and process information in order to operate effectively in *all* areas of the curriculum. The Library Association has published a set of descriptions of generic skills (Table 5.3), which illustrates the 'integrated' nature of career learning, in so far as the information processing skills learned in other curriculum areas should be transferable to careers work, and vice versa.

Table 5.3 Generic learning skills.

Traditionally, library skills ... and information skills sessions concentrated on finding information, with little emphasis on defining what information was required or on how to use and evaluate it effectively ... The following learning skills form the basis of the learning process required by the new curricula.

Planning skills	Planning skills are the essential pre-requisite for any research task. Brainstorming, appropriate question framing and keyword identification are essential skills that require practice at this stage of the learning process.
Location and gathering skills	Locating and gathering ... are fundamental skills, which are too often assumed, yet require practice at increasingly sophisticated levels ...
Selection and appraisal skills	Pupils need to develop critical, evaluative thinking skills ... learning how to identify relevant, up-to-date and authoritative information, available within school or from outside sources, and in detecting any bias or inaccuracy ... A wide range of resources needs to be consulted, compared and appraised, to ensure that hypotheses and conclusions are formed upon the widest possible knowledge base.
Organisation and recording skills	Dealing with the information that has been gathered and selected.
Communication and realisation skills	Communicating the results of any enquiry, or realising a design or composition in any practical subject, in a way that demonstrates true understanding and interpretation is one of the most difficult learning skills that has to be attained.
Evaluation skills	Evaluating the learning process, the information content and its form of presentation is an equally important stage of any assignment ...

(Adapted from '**National Curriculum and Learning Skills**', *The Library Association 1991.)*

The framework outlined in Table 5.3 can be used to help students develop information search and processing skills by using the careers library. It can also be used in the context of other information sources, such as those generated by the life history approach described later in this Section.

Setting up an assignment for using the careers library, based upon four 40-minute PSHE lessons during Year 9.

	Key tasks
Session One: Groups of students from Year 9 each attended an 'introduction to the careers library' session, which was delivered by the school's careers adviser. This dealt with the purpose of the library, the classification system, range and type of resource materials, access and support. **Session Two:** Students completed a questionnaire about their interests, which generated several career areas for their forthcoming careers library research. Using the CLCI index, each student identified which categories contained information they might need. **Session Three:** Students worked in groups to devise a careers library search strategy. With help from their tutors and visiting careers adviser, students decided which resources they would like to use, and the main questions to which they wanted answers.	**Prior to library research** Students should: ● familiarise themselves with the location, range and structure of careers library resources ● familiarise themselves with the careers library classification system ● formulate key questions ● identify key words and search terms ● develop a search strategy ● identify outputs – what do they want/need to gain from the exercise?
Students had a two week period in which to undertake their library search, during lunch periods and tutor periods. Tutors had been briefed and following their own staff development session in the careers library, they were quite able to support students who needed individual help. The careers adviser was also on hand during several lunch periods to provide additional support.	**Support during library research activity** The careers co-ordinator should: ● discuss, agree and organise availability of tutors, careers advisers, and/or careers librarians, as appropriate.

Session Four: Each student was expected to write a short report on their mini research project. Four students were asked to give a verbal report to the class. They were given the following framework:
 	
1. What did you want to find out?
   ● *Did you succeed? If so what went well?*
   ● *Did you run into problems? What were they and did you overcome them?*
2. What resources did you find the most useful? Give some examples.
3. What did you think about the information you found out?
   ● *Was it accurate and up-to-date?*
   ● *Was it relevant?*
   ● *How have you been able to use it?*
4. How could the resources be improved?
	Follow-up and review
	
	All of the Library Association skills (Table 5.3) could be used as part of the review, but more generally students should think about:
	
	● **search strategies** – how effective/ ineffective were they? What alternative strategies might students use in future?
	
	● **process problems** – What worked well? What proved frustrating?
	
	● the **value of the information** retrieved and what action might follow

Varied Approaches to Information Search and Processing

This final section describes three different examples of information gathering and processing. These examples place the student in the *centre* of the process, rather than in the role of recipient of 'handed down' information generated by other people and agencies.

Guided Self-Study Approaches

Self-study guides have been around for some time in one guise or another, but have only recently been applied to careers education and guidance. Examples include:

- *Career Guides* (1994), Kent County Council and Network Educational Press
- *Career Planning Guide* (1996), Careers Enterprise Group
- Edwards in *Careers Education and Guidance: Developing Professional Practice* (1995), Kogan Page

These materials are intended to provide students with a structured and sequential approach to enquiry, which helps them to generate and utilise information related to any one of a number of career themes, such as 'choices at 18', or 'preparing for interviews'.

Self-study guides can be designed to lead a student through an enquiry that will engage him/her in elements of sensing and sifting and/or classifying (see Table 5.2 and Figure 5.1). They also provide the student with a strategy for locating, processing and evaluating specific information that is most directly relevant to their concerns. In addition, emphasis is placed on reflection and action. Students can use the supported self-study approach individually or linked into the tutorial system, which can provide added support and feedback (Edwards, 1995).

Although self-study resources are commercially available, schools should be able to produce materials tailored to their own particular needs. Access to desktop publishing programmes is extremely useful for this purpose.

Life History or Biographical Approaches

Life history or biographical approaches can provide a rich source of 'local' material, which is 'close' enough to students to have authenticity and a voice of its own. This approach involves students in some field work of their own, in which they may gather data from interviews or from other available biographical sources (different media sources, such as fiction and documentary, can be invaluable – Fox, 1995). For example, members of a GNVQ group might prepare to interview members from their family or community about aspects of their experiences from working life, past and present. The students are subsequently able to process and record their findings, to interrogate and interpret the information and to relate it to their own understanding and perceptions about 'work, self and role'.

Using Authoring Programmes

'Authoring' programmes can be used to record and display information and experiences. There are a number of authoring programmes currently on the market, each offering different degrees of sophistication (and complexity). They allow the user to create a series of 'story-boards', which are linked pages of information, potentially containing text, graphics, audio, stills and video clips.

Examples of such multi-media authoring packages include:

- Macromedia Director
- Authorware
- Iconauthor
- Adobe Premier
- Toolbook
- Hyperstudio

The ability to import frames from the Internet, or from a digital camera or video, and integrate them with spoken or written material, offers considerable scope for teachers and students to develop high-value IT skills by representing career-relevant information in the form of multi-media presentations or teaching and learning resources. These programmes also offer exciting scope for collaborative work between IT and careers departments.

Some innovative examples of new technologies applied to careers guidance work are summarised below (list continues on page 76). Each of these seven development projects has been funded through the DfEE, from whom more information is available (see bibliography).

1. *The Virtual Reception*

    From: Birmingham Careers Service Partnership Ltd.

    Project Aim: To develop a 'computer-based reception' that can interpret the guidance needs of clients and assist them in finding appropriate resources to fulfil their needs.

2. *Cambridgeshire Careers Exchange*

    From: Cambridge Training and Development Ltd. (CTAD) and Cambridgeshire Careers Guidance Ltd. (CCG)

    Project Aim: To create a network-based system that will allow guidance professionals and young people (14+) to make productive use of technology in the guidance process, so enabling a more effective use of interview time (see Figure 5.2).

3. *Voice Activated Computers to Produce Action Plans in Schools*

    From: County Durham Careers Service

    Project Aim: To use speech recognition software on portable computers to produce action plans within schools.

4. *Careers Guidance at a Distance*

    From: JIIG-CAL Ltd.

    Project Aim: To evaluate the effectiveness of video conferencing and alternative approaches to giving clients access to careers advisers in remote locations.

Figure 5.2

The Cambridgeshire Careers Exchange – developed by Cambridge Training and Development Ltd and Cambridgeshire Careers Guidance Ltd

The Cambridgeshire Careers Exchange has been developed to give young people and staff in schools front-end access to a range of services – the pilot system provides:

- access to Email
- a conference facility (text only)
- a notice board
- a job shop linked to the CSRS (Careers Service Record System)
- library of electronic KeyClips

The core component of the pilot system is the action-planning tool. The system also contains an Experience Exchange, which offers students the opportunity to create audio-visual slide shows of their experiences.

The system is designed to be used as part of an integrated careers guidance programme. It can be used as it stands, or customised with new features, or linked to existing software.

The network created for the pilot uses one central fileserver and eight remote sites, four in schools and four in careers offices.

Notice Board

Provided that their own computer is connected to the central fileserver, careers teachers, careers advisers and students can send information that they want to publicise to a much wider audience – for example, details about a careers convention, open days or any other event or important piece of information.

Action

This section consists of an action-planning preparatory activity and contains six sections, each with questions for the student to complete on screen. Sections cover areas such as family situation, what the student is good at, personal style, exam forecasts, activities outside of school, and so on. A print out can be produced and taken to the careers interview or given to the careers adviser in advance. It is seen mainly as a discussion starter.

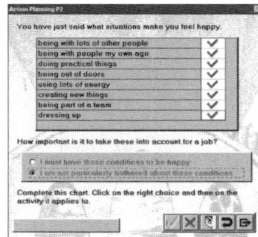

Job Shop

Cambridgeshire Careers Guidance Ltd have a computerised system for job vacancies, which are accessible through this part of the programme. Students can search for vacancies under industry classifications to identify jobs of interest. Full information can be obtained from the careers service. Course information can also be managed in this way.

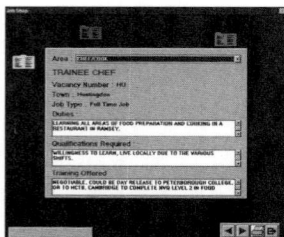

Mail

This is an Email facility.

Launch

This has not yet been activated but will eventually give users access to the Internet.

Main Menu Screen

Users input their name, then a chosen password.

Library

This allows users access to a full set of electronic KeyClips, which are information pages covering a wide range of occupational information. The various slide shows used in the Experience Exchange can also be accessed.

Experience Exchange

This consists of a series of slide shows of different people's experiences of career choice and decision-making. The slide shows take the form of mini case studies and include examples of students' experiences of dealing with university applications, applying for a GAP year, dealing with parental pressure, entering engineering as a women, doing the Youth Award Scheme, etc. These are audio-visual presentations and utilise photographs, cartoons, drawings, sound recordings and text.

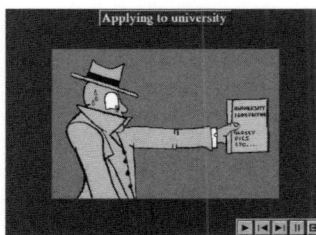

Reception

This contains introductory slide shows using audio and visual materials, which describe the programme to new users. It also suggests where students should go for further help – to their careers co-ordinators and careers advisers, for example.

Meet

This is a conference facility which can be open (so that everyone can read what has been written) or closed (so that it can only be read by careers co-ordinators and/or career advisers). For example, a careers adviser might start a 'conference' by writing about her impressions of a recent university visit. Other users can respond to the discussion, which begins to take the shape of a tree structure. This allows users to respond to any part of the discussion they like.

Reproduced by kind permission of Cambridge Training and Development Ltd and Cambridgeshire Careers Guidance Ltd.

5. *Guidance Access Points (or Virtual Careers Centres)*

   From: Tyneside Careers

   Project Aim: To develop and evaluate 'Guidance Access Points' (GAPs) in locations around Tyneside and enhance guidance by reducing unnecessary travel and waiting time.

6. *Applications of Multi-Media Technology to the Careers Education and Guidance Needs of Pupils with Moderate Learning Difficulties*

   From: Future Steps Ltd.

   Project Aim: To investigate where multi-media resources could be used successfully in order to enhance the provision of careers education and guidance for pupils with moderate learning difficulties.

7. *Effective Use of Computer Technology in Careers Guidance*

   From: Scottish Council for Research in Education (SCRE) and JIIG-CAL Ltd.

   Project Aim: To evaluate the impact of new technology on careers guidance in schools, with a view to identifying the factors that lead to effective use and best practice.

Action Points

- [ ] **Devise workable strategies for maintaining your careers library or resource area.**

- [ ] **Introduce an annual review and audit of the careers resources available to your students.**

- [ ] **Ensure that your resource materials meet the minimum criteria for good practice.**

- [ ] **Develop information resources that are innovative and varied.**

- [ ] **Review the range of opportunities given to students in order for them to learn and practice information processing skills.**

- [ ] **Create opportunities for students to learn and apply information processing skills as part of their careers learning.**

Section Six

Experiences of Work

> **In Section Six, we learn that:**
>
> ☛ **Work-related activities contribute to careers education and guidance, economic and industrial understanding and the overall education of students.**
>
> ☛ **Work-related activities make use of experiential learning approaches.**
>
> ☛ **A planned and progressive programme drawing on a full range of work-related activities should be devised as part of the curriculum.**
>
> ☛ **Work-related activities help to make labour market information more accessible.**

This Section looks at the reasons why experiences of work are such an essential element of careers provision. A key reason for their success is that they use learning processes that are highly accessible to students, such as experiential learning. The Section investigates ways of maximising the benefits of various work-related activities, and discusses important issues related to the management of experiences of work in the careers education and guidance programme.

The Contribution of Work-Related Activities

Interest in 'work-related activities' and the 'work-related curriculum' mushroomed in the early years of the Technical and Vocational Education Initiative (Extension) (1987–1997). One of the best working-definitions of the place of 'work' in the school curriculum was published by the Centre for Education and Industry at the University of Warwick (1992):

> *'Work-related' teaching and learning involves a collaboration between schools and employers to*
> - *improve the transition of young people from school to adult and working life by raising standards in careers education and guidance (i.e. education for industry)*
> - *improve young people's economic and industrial understanding (i.e. education about industry)*
> - *raise standards across the whole curriculum by providing a resource, environment and context in order to improve the motivation and attainment of all students (i.e. education through industry)*

The idea of education for, about and through industry is a useful frame of reference. It makes clear that the rationale for education–business links extends across the whole curriculum. This has implications for school managers, who need to ensure a coherent, planned and progressive approach to providing students with work-related experiences within their overall education. What curriculum managers sometimes overlook is that *all* work-related activities have a *de facto* potential to contribute to the career learning and development of students. Schools need to ensure that this potential is not missed.

The case for delivering aspects of careers education and guidance through work-related activities focuses on the benefits to learners, described in the following sections.

Accessible Learning

Work-related activities are closer to everyday learning situations. Students do not need formal academic skills before they can start to benefit. Honey and Mumford (1982) identified four main learning styles: activists (eager to learn from new experiences), pragmatists (practical problem-solvers), theorists (happiest working with concepts, models and theories) and reflectors (preferring to think before acting). In terms of individuals' preferred learning styles, work-related activities particularly benefit students classified as activists or pragmatists.

Work-related activities are also memorable. Two weeks' work experience, a two-day *Insight into Industry* course or a day-visit to a manufacturing plant evoke powerful memories which will last long after hundreds of forty-minute lessons have been forgotten!

Relevant Learning

From early childhood, children learn about the work that adults do around them. They experience a sense of wonder at the work adults do and the equipment they use, which is sometimes lost in adolescence and adulthood. Their enthusiasm for work and sense of anticipation, once aroused, can be a powerful motivator.

Realistic Learning

Most work-related activities involve direct, first-hand experience of the world of work. Even simulations aim to capture this quality of immediate experience. This can have a considerable impact on students' learning.

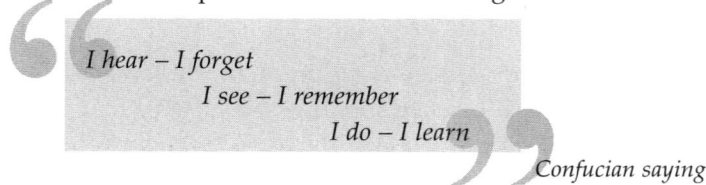

> *I hear – I forget*
> *I see – I remember*
> *I do – I learn*
> Confucian saying

One of the most compelling arguments for work-related activities is the opportunity they afford for students to take on adult roles and responsibilities. Getting to work on time, following instructions and dealing face-to-face with clients and customers are typical activities on work-experience. Work-related activities enable students to rehearse adult roles and responsibilities in a relatively safe environment.

Experiential Learning

Community- and work-experience are examples of 'learning in the raw'. They often stimulate intense emotional experiences, which can produce some of the most profound learning in students, about themselves and the world of work. Kolb (1984) has attempted to capture the nature of this process in the experiential learning cycle (Figure 6.1).

Figure 6.1 Experiential learning cycle (after Kolb).

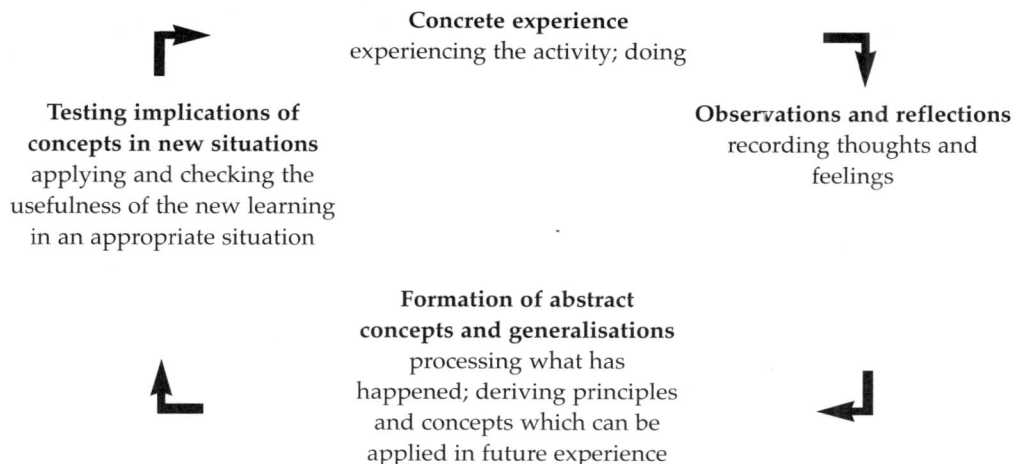

Concrete experience
experiencing the activity; doing

Observations and reflections
recording thoughts and
feelings

**Formation of abstract
concepts and generalisations**
processing what has
happened; deriving principles
and concepts which can be
applied in future experience

**Testing implications of
concepts in new situations**
applying and checking the
usefulness of the new learning
in an appropriate situation

As the cycle in Figure 6.1 shows, simply having the experience is not enough to generate effective learning. Students need time and a suitable process for reviewing and reflecting on their experiences. Sadly, this time is not always made available, especially when the activity is squeezed in just before a holiday. A drawback of experiential learning is that it does require more time than a didactic approach; but experiential learning reaches the parts that other methods cannot reach!

Types of Activities

Table 6.1 gives an idea of the range of work-related activities that can be incorporated into the careers education and guidance programme.

Table 6.1   Types of work-related activities.

Workplace learning	Simulations
● work-experience	● role plays
● work-shadowing	● business games
● visits	● mini enterprises
● industrial-based and school-based projects	● simulated work-experience
	● task weeks
Working with business partners	**Resources and materials**
● mentoring and compacts	● information packs
● visitors in the classroom	● videos
● mock interviews	● software
● careers conventions	● competitions
● industry days/weeks	

Compacts are contracts agreed between students, schools and opportunity providers (e.g. employers, colleges). They offer benefits to students (e.g. offers of places or employment) in return for improved effort (e.g. regular attendance at school).

Labour Market Information

One of the main benefits of work-related careers education and guidance is the contribution it can make to students' knowledge of opportunities in education, training and work. *LMI Matters* (1996) defined labour market information (LMI) as information about:

- the nature of work
- education, training and qualifications
- economics, industries, sectors and jobs
- demography (population changes, age structure, etc.)

The information can be local, regional, national or international.

Schools are increasingly finding new and imaginative ways to use LMI with students as the following examples show.

Case Studies

Industry trail

A small group of Year 10 students in a residential special school for students with emotional and behavioural difficulties devised an industry trail around part of the local town for Year 9 students to follow. They planned the route of the trail by using maps and guide books, and by talking to the careers adviser. After selecting places of interest, they walked the route themselves to check it out, and to help them write the commentary and questions for the Year 9s to answer. Geographical and mathematical skills were involved in working out distances, times needed to get from one place to the next, and grid references. IT skills were also needed in order to produce the industry trail leaflet.

International communication

Some GNVQ Intermediate students exchanged information on leisure and tourism with students in Greece and the Netherlands by fax and Email.

'Transition Team'

Some Year 10 students took part in an innovative six-week scheme to enable small groups of students to research their post 16 options by visiting providers of opportunities. The Transition Team's project applied the principles of enterprise education and co-operative learning to careers education and guidance. At the end of the project, each group presented its findings to the rest of the class.

Effective Careers Education and Guidance

Work-experience database

During their work-experience placements, Year 10 students collected information about the composition of the work force, vacancy prospects and opportunities for school leavers. On their return to school, they entered this and additional information (e.g. their own details, the occupation undertaken and the correct industrial classification for the organisation) in a database. They were then able to analyse features of the local economy, employment trends and prospects for school leavers. Their analysis of work-experience placements by gender and occupational grouping produced an animated discussion about the incidence of stereotyping.

Local issues

As part of a careers module in Personal and Social Education, small groups of Year 10 students undertook local area profiling using information that the school librarian had collected in topic folders. Topics included: employment, industry, the environment, health and social care, leisure and tourism, education and local government. Students analysed the newspaper cuttings, leaflets and reports in their topic folders, along with other information that they found by making enquiries. Each group then presented a report outlining up to three issues or concerns for young people, related to their topic area. From these lists of issues, the whole class agreed what were the top three problems (which involved some re-grouping and defining of issues) and suggested ways of tackling them.

Maximising the Benefits of Activities

A recent study of work-related careers education and guidance activities, published in a DfEE-funded report into effective teaching and learning in work-related contexts in 16 schools (Harris et al, 1997), identified the following features of good practice:

1. Best practice was generally to be found in those schools where there was a coherent philosophical approach to teaching and learning about the world of work, which was clearly articulated and shared.

2. A careers convention clearly fulfils the function of information dissemination but two schools used the occasion specifically to reinforce relationships with Adults-Other-than-Teachers (AOTs). One school also deliberately invited ex-pupils with local business connections thus providing role models for the current cohort.

3. Several schools ran some kind of main event where the timetable was suspended for whole groups to take part in business simulations with AOTs. Such events might be called 'Insight into Industry', 'Community Week' or 'Industry Week' and several of the students interviewed identified these events as occasions that helped them not only to develop skills like team-working, but also to firm up on personal career plans.

4. Two schools in the sample ran ACE days ('Aiming for a College Education'). These events, often sponsored by industry, used AOTs to familiarise pupils, through activities, with the worlds of further and higher education.

5. As students developed the knowledge, skills and attitudes they required to manage their own careers effectively they were often offered additional opportunities to support their development. One such opportunity was work-shadowing, which

often took place in the early stages of secondary school and was used to develop general ideas about the workplace. Another opportunity offered to each student was a mock interview, usually held in Year 11. One school operated a Job Shop in which all Year 11 students were required to apply for a job, and were interviewed by an AOT.

6. Where teaching styles were more didactic in nature there was some evidence to suggest that students were less well prepared for the working environment.

7. One school had developed a progressive careers education and guidance programme, which began in year 7 with a 'What's my line?' event. As part of this event, AOTs were brought into school to take part in an exercise devised to combat sex stereotyping.

8. The best schools used their careers officers in wider AOT roles across the work-related curriculum, to great effect.

9. Part of any effective careers education and guidance programme ought to be concerned with providing students with a realistic picture of what the world of work will be like in the future.

Which work-related activities contribute significantly to the effectiveness of careers education and guidance in your school?

Do any of the above activities already take place in your school?

Do the activities described above suggest any useful ideas for things that you could do differently or for new things that you could do?

Maximising the benefits of activities involves careful curriculum management to deal with issues such as relevance, access and participation, coherence and continuity, sequencing and progression.

The criteria listed in Table 6.2, based on a local education–business partnership scheme, should help you to address the issue of quality in work-related careers education and guidance activities.

Table 6.2 Criteria for assessing quality in work-related activities.

Worthwhile learning outcomes for students	Students should make gains in their own personal, social and career development, as well as in their enhanced awareness of the world of work.
Effective curriculum management	The co-ordinator should provide leadership and curriculum management, and contribute to staff development; the co-ordinator should ensure that activities are underpinned by equality of opportunity.
Effective participation of an appropriate range of staff	Appropriate contributions should be made by staff, as a result of delegation or team-work e.g. tutors visiting students on work-experience.
Effective partnership with parents, businesses and education–business support agencies	Schools should work closely with parents, business and community organisations, and education–business support agencies such as the careers service and education–business partnerships.
Efficient administration and resource management	Schools should make best use of the resources available for work-related careers education and guidance activities.

Action Points

☐ Review the place of work-related activities within your careers education and guidance programme.

☐ Evaluate your work-experience scheme as an experiential learning opportunity for your students.

☐ Examine the use of labour market information in your careers education and guidance programme and how it might be further developed.

☐ Complete the activities based on the study by Harris et al to help you identify possible next steps.

☐ Assess the quality of your school's work-related activities using the criteria in Table 6.2.

Section Seven

Contributing to School Effectiveness and Improvement

In Section Seven, we learn that:

☞ *Senior managers and governors have a key role at the strategic level in the pro-active management of careers education and guidance.*

☞ *Good careers education and guidance provision is the hallmark of an effective school and it can contribute to school improvement.*

☞ *The contribution of careers education and guidance to school effectiveness and improvement can be developed by attention to first destination returns, accreditation of careers learning, whole-school policy on guidance and equal opportunity issues.*

This Section looks at the contribution of well-managed, high profile careers education and guidance to school effectiveness (achieving desired outcomes) and improvement (achieving those outcomes more effectively through the successful management of change). The commitment to high quality careers education and guidance starts with senior management and governors.

The Role of Senior Managers and Governors

Careers work must be managed at the strategic level. Strategic planning involves knowing what goal to achieve, being able to justify moving in that direction, and then finding the best way to reach the goal. For schools, the goals are complex and often contradictory, but no school can afford to ignore careers education and guidance as a strategic priority. Its importance stems from Section One of the 1988 Education Act, which requires schools to prepare students for:

> *... the opportunities, responsibilities and experiences of adult life.*

Careers education and guidance has a major part to play in achieving this goal. Senior managers and governors can help to maximise the contribution of careers work to school effectiveness and improvement by:

- **clarifying** the place of careers education and guidance in the school's aims and mission; and communicating this commitment appropriately e.g. in a statement of student entitlement, in an entry in the prospectus for parents, in a policy and guidelines document for staff

- **budgeting** for the provision of careers education and guidance; and ensuring that resources are sufficient and that the best use is made of them

- **selecting** careers staff to lead and manage the careers education and guidance programme; and promoting their professional development through training and appraisal. As well as general support from the senior management team, the careers co-ordinator should have a line manager for specific support. Some schools have had success in identifying a 'buddy' or 'link' governor who takes a special interest in supporting the school's careers work

- **helping to plan** the careers education and guidance programme; and supporting its implementation

- **monitoring** the careers education and guidance programme; and ensuring that regular review and evaluation takes place e.g. through equal opportunities monitoring

- **promoting** continuous improvement in the careers education and guidance provision e.g. through target-setting and development planning

These needs have been highlighted in a recent survey of careers education and guidance in schools by OFSTED (1995), as shown in the following extract.

In order to improve the management and administration of careers education and guidance, schools need to:

- clarify aims and devise a rationale, policy and programme for all students

- bring together key players on a regular basis to agree priorities and strategies

- review the timing and use made of PSE for providing the careers education and guidance programme

- refer to recent publications ... which give good advice and support for planning

- ensure that sufficient time and resources are made available to deliver what has been agreed

- introduce more systematic quality assurance measures

- adjust written job descriptions as necessary and ensure that careers co-ordinators have regular meetings with designated line managers

- ensure that SLAs (service level or partnership agreements) reflect school needs alongside the priorities of the Careers Service

- review teachers' in-service needs in relation to the curriculum, making use of the GEST arrangements

As well as the statutory obligation to ensure equality of opportunity in the careers education and guidance provision (see page 91), senior managers and governors also have the following responsibilities.

Secondary schools must include information in the school prospectus about their provision for careers education, guidance and work-experience.

DfEE Circular 12/96

Secondary schools must provide a programme of careers education for Years 9 to 11, access to guidance materials and Ö careers information, and access to the careers service.

Education Act 1997

Are the senior management and governors in your school fully aware of their potentially powerful role in careers education and guidance, and therefore in school effectiveness and improvement?

How could you help to clarify and emphasise the importance of this role to them?

The Link to School Effectiveness and Improvement

We have already suggested that effectiveness is about getting desired results or outcomes, and that improvement refers to the school's capacity to enhance these outcomes through the successful management of change. This hints at the possibility of a dual role for careers education and guidance as:

1. a **contributory factor** in the achievement of other valued outcomes associated with an effective and improving school

2. an **essential component** of an effective and improving school in its own right

Consider the range of possibilities for defining an effective and improving school:

- a school's exam results are better than might be expected, given its intake, and the school is continuing to extend this value-added benefit

- a school achieves, and then exceeds, the National Targets for Education and Training

- a school achieves impressive results in the assessment of key skills and can demonstrate a year-on-year improvement

- a school's SATs results show that students are achieving higher than expected levels of attainment in National Curriculum subjects and the gains are progressive

Could careers education and guidance be a significant factor in helping schools to make these gains? According to the OFSTED model for whole-school inspection (see Section Twelve), careers education and guidance impacts directly on the overall educational standards achieved by the school. *Better Choices: Putting the Principles into Practice* (DfEE, 1995) suggested a range of possible benefits, as outlined over the page.

Effective careers work helps students to succeed. It also helps schools and colleges achieve their broader aims, particularly in the following areas.

1. Effective careers work **raises aspirations** by:
   - broadening individuals' horizons and increasing their knowledge and understanding of all the available opportunities in education, training and employment
   - encouraging individuals to explore options they may not have considered or had assumed would not be open to them
   - challenging occupational stereotypes
   - providing impartial advice and guidance

2. Effective careers work **raises levels of motivation and achievement** by:
   - promoting the development of self-esteem and self-confidence, and the acquisition of techniques, such as action-planning, which help individuals to take increasing control over the direction of their personal and career development
   - relating learning and curriculum content to future opportunities, including the world of work
   - using teaching and learning styles that give learners responsibility for, and experience of, problem-solving and decision-making
   - helping individuals to develop skills associated with success in education, training, employment and self-employment (e.g. reliability, team-work, taking responsibility)
   - helping individuals to develop the skills and flexibility needed to manage changing career opportunities

3. Effective careers work **improves success, attendance and retention rates** by:
   - providing objective and impartial guidance and counselling before enrolment, in preparation for other key transition points and in response to individual needs
   - linking individuals to programmes that are relevant and meet their requirements

Another way in which careers education and guidance contributes to overall effectiveness and improvement is as a catalyst for curriculum change. Careers work is a curriculum activity that straddles the boundary between the school and the world outside. It is a conduit for introducing new influences, contacts and resources into the school. Senior managers and governors can harness careers initiatives to provide the necessary support and pressure for change.

How could you use the careers education and guidance programme to introduce new influences in your school?

What influences, contacts or resources might you wish to introduce?

The Hallmark of an Effective and Improving School

At the national level, the target-setting measures used to assess effectiveness have been limited to a narrow range of indicators that emphasise students' examination achievements and performance in basic skills.

In some area networks, schools have identified broader measures of effectiveness. A good example is the Birmingham Secondary Guarantee drawn up by the LEA and its partner schools (1996). This Guarantee includes a careers entitlement and several targets related to careers education and guidance.

Careers Entitlement
As part of his/her careers entitlement, each student should experience a build up of careers awareness throughout the secondary phase, and receive the best advice concerning destinations on leaving and preparation for future change and development.

Targets of Process or Experience
By the age of 16 each pupil should have participated in a quality work-experience placement as part of a planned programme of work-related activities.

Targets of Outcome
By the age of 16 every pupil should have produced an accredited Record of Achievement, which incorporates a career plan and an IT-driven project.

A successful transition will be attempted for each pupil to the next stage of continuing education or training/employment.

Research is needed to identify the key careers education and guidance processes and outcomes that contribute most to school effectiveness and improvement. Much work still remains to be done on how the factors affecting school effectiveness and improvement interrelate. Areas of careers work that could provide a starting point for such research include:

- **career management skills**, such as self-reliance, decision-making, problem-solving, initiative and enterprise, self-presentation, assertiveness and negotiation, organisation and time management, research and information handling. Through the careers education and guidance programme, students should acquire these transferable skills, which they can apply across broad areas of personal capability

- **progression** in education, training or employment. Careers education and guidance promotes knowledge of through-routes in the qualifications and selection maze. It helps to reduce inefficient job- or course-seeking behaviour by students and inefficient recruitment behaviour by opportunity providers

- **successful choices and transitions**. Careers education and guidance in schools should help students to cope successfully with taking the next steps in their careers

In your school, what careers education and guidance processes and outcomes do you think significantly affect school effectiveness and improvement?

Increasing School Effectiveness and Improvement

Using First Destination Returns

Schools and careers services can combine their resources to collect data on the first destinations of leavers, in order to help evaluate the contribution of the careers education and guidance programme to school effectiveness and improvement. Once such an evaluation has been made, plans to enhance the contribution can be made.

The census date for collecting information about first destinations is 31st October for students leaving school in the summer. Schools may point out, quite rightly, that this data has limitations: some students may still be filling in time until they can get started. Longitudinal studies, which follow-up changes and moves in the following years, would perhaps be more revealing of the impact of the school on students' career prospects (although school effects would be hard to disentangle from other influences). Provided the limitations of the data are kept in mind, the analysis of first destinations can provide the school with useful feedback on its effectiveness. This is especially true when the school has access to data on its own students going back over a number of years, as well as comparative data showing local, regional and national trends.

The following data on first destinations could be collected:

- student's name
- student's gender, ethnic background and special educational needs
- student's level of educational attainment
- student's status e.g. full-time or part-time, student, trainee, employee, unemployed or volunteer
- student's destination e.g. school sixth form, college, National Traineeship, Modern Apprenticeship, job, unemployed at 16+
- titles and levels of subjects, courses or job

If you have such first destinations data available, you could interrogate it in the following ways:

- **Have students managed to make progress e.g. on to the next level?**
- **Have students managed to make moves that are as good as can be expected in the current state of the education, training and labour markets?**
- **Does the data indicate that the school's careers education and guidance curriculum is relevant and appropriate? Are any adjustments required?**

Seeking Accredited Outcomes

Accrediting learning in careers work can help to broaden the base of achievement by students at the school. Accreditation schemes can help to make the provision a more coherent experience for students; but it can also distort and fragment what is offered (see Section Three). The *Report on Effective Teaching and Learning in Work-Related Contexts* (Harris et al, 1996) found that schools which could not compete successfully in the league tables of examination results were more likely to seek accreditation in areas of students' personal and social development.

> *A substantial majority of our sample was made up of schools that were not achieving high positions in academic league tables. Although they were invariably trying to address this issue, it was recognised that local socio-economic factors meant that a general improvement in academic performance would be difficult. When this was coupled with unpromising local employment prospects, schools seemed to be concentrating their efforts on ensuring that whatever their students achieved was acknowledged, recorded and had optimum use made of it. Thus, there was an enhanced emphasis on careers education and guidance, work-experience and accreditation through records of achievement and other methods of certification (Award Scheme Development and Accreditation Network [ASDAN] Awards, Compact, etc.).*

Accreditation schemes for careers education and guidance can benefit students across the ability range, and, therefore, have something to offer all students in all schools (see Section Three).

Does accredited learning in careers work take place in your school?

How do you think accredited learning could contribute to the effectiveness and improvement of your school?

Improving Guidance

The achievement of students is directly related to the quality of guidance provided by the school. It is helpful to plan the guidance programme and review arrangements around three stages of provision:

1. **on entry** – e.g. guidance provided during initial visits and during induction
2. **on programme** – e.g. continuing guidance provision, which helps students to make progress and choose options on their courses
3. **on exit** – e.g. help with making applications, and provision of post-results counselling

Does your school have a policy on guidance that covers personal, education and career guidance?

Seeking Equality of Opportunity

Careers work can contribute significantly to the achievement of the school's goals in relation to equality of opportunity.

The school's policy on careers education and guidance should make explicit its relationship to the school's policy on equality of opportunity. Students are also entitled to equality of opportunity within the careers programme:

> *There should be no discrimination against any pupil on the grounds of race, sex or disability in ... giving guidance and work-experience.*

> *Sex Discrimination Act 1975, Race Relations Act 1976, DfEE Circular 12/96*

The careers education and guidance programme should help students to understand the case for equality of opportunity in careers and work as well as helping them to operate within an equal opportunities code of conduct. This can be achieved by providing some or all of the following opportunities:

- investigating the provision of equality of opportunity in workplaces e.g. on work-experience
- raising awareness of the drawbacks of stereotyped thinking in subject and occupational choice
- providing role models to raise aspirations further
- discussing social and moral issues in relation to discrimination in education, training and work opportunities
- studying careers materials, such as job advertisements and recruitment literature, to expose biased or insensitive information which presents a narrow range of lifestyles, ignores or diminishes groups of people, and perpetuates stereotypes

Case Study

A group of students studied a selection of newspaper advertisements for school leaver vacancies. They immediately criticised the sexual innuendo and stereotyping in an advertisement for a computer store manager. Other advertisements needed more careful scrutiny before students spotted what was objectionable about them. A High Street retailer, for example, showed a picture of four of its management trainees. At first glance, the gender and ethnic balance appeared acceptable; but the two men in the picture were standing separately and apart while the two women were leaning against each other. This led to an interesting discussion about the stereotyping of the management styles of women and men.

How could the careers education and guidance programme in your school be changed to improve achievement of goals relating to equality of opportunity?

Action Points

☐ Review the practical arrangements for the overall management of careers education and guidance in your school.

☐ Decide how you should respond to the recommendations in the 1995 OFSTED report (page 86) if you have not already done so.

☐ Assess the contribution of careers education and guidance to your school's effectiveness and improvement.

☐ Plan how to make better use of first destination information as a measure of your school's effectiveness in helping students to make progress in their lives.

☐ Monitor the arrangements for ensuring equality of opportunity in and through careers education and guidance.

Section Eight

The Role of the Careers Co-ordinator

In Section Eight, we learn that:

☞ *The careers co-ordinator's role involves a wide range of management skills and abilities, even if the role is not internally recognised as a management position.*

☞ *The role of careers co-ordinator is not static. The concept of 'career' has recently undergone important changes, which should influence our understanding of careers education and guidance and what must be provided for students.*

☞ *There is a distinction, and sometimes a conflict, between the needs of the student and the needs of the organisation. Part of the co-ordinator's role is to reconcile the differences in the needs of each, or at least keep them in balance.*

☞ *Four key roles are suggested for the careers co-ordinator, viewed from a student-centred perspective:*

    1. resources and information manager

    2. co-ordinator of learning opportunities and activities

    3. interpreter and advocate

    4. communicator and networker

☞ *Key tasks for the careers co-ordinator are summarised under seven headings, which can form the basis of an audit and development plan.*

☞ *Developing self and role is also important for the careers co-ordinator – consolidating existing strengths and developing new skills and abilities.*

☞ *A reflective approach to practice can greatly improve effectiveness.*

☞ *Working with others interested in careers work is an important dimension of professional growth and learning.*

Few teachers who have be given the responsibility to co-ordinate careers work in school or college doubt that a wide range of management skills are required in order to exercise the role effectively, even if the role is not recognised in the school as a management post. In some schools, perhaps a minority, a senior teacher performs the co-ordinator's role. In other instances, the co-ordinator may also occupy other management-related roles within the school. Yet many careers co-ordinators find themselves rather more isolated from the 'main channels' of power and influence, and therefore have to find methods of managing the role and responsibilities without the designated authority and resources commonly attached to 'conventional' management positions.

The role of the careers co-ordinator is not static. The virtual demise of the youth labour market, and the vastly increased number of students remaining in post-compulsory education and entering higher education, have brought about important changes to both the meaning and shape of young people's 'careers'. This fact has implications for what careers co-ordinators do, and means they must be able to respond readily to external changes and trends.

The aim of this Section is to explore particular aspects of the co-ordinators 'management' role, which is affected by both internal and external factors as well as by students' changing needs.

The Changing Role of the Careers Co-ordinator

Until the late 1970s and early 1980s, the majority of students left school and entered employment at 16. Therefore, careers education and guidance was concerned mainly with preparing large numbers of students for the labour market. In recent years, we have had to revise radically our understanding of the concept of a 'career'. The idea of pursuing a single occupation that is stable and possibly progressive is one that far fewer can aspire to. Roberts (1996), for example, has recently suggested that young people now have individual patterns in education leading to very different biographies by their early twenties. Careers education and guidance, in his terms, must be customised to the needs of each individual, who is likely to need:

> *...recurrent guidance for prolonged transitions throughout his/her working life.*

Elliot (1996) has similarly argued that given the collapse of occupational structures and hierarchies, schools are now loosing their traditional allocative functions and therefore they must develop a curriculum that helps young people construct some kind of future for themselves. This poses a real challenge for schools, and especially careers co-ordinators, given the limited time typically allocated to careers work in terms of curriculum space and non-contact time (Cleaton, 1993).

Some of theses changes have highlighted the distinction, and sometimes the conflict, between the actions that careers co-ordinators may need to undertake on behalf of their students, and the actions that may be required of them from an organisational perspective. A large part of the co-ordinator's role is given to keeping these two pressures in a state of healthy tension.

Is it possible to uphold the view that student's needs are of paramount importance while remaining in step with the goals and aspirations of your school?

It is unrealistic to expect the careers co-ordinator alone to have the capacity or ability to meet every student's career planning needs. The role is too often marginal and unsupported, with insufficient resources available to discharge the full range of responsibilities and tasks involved. Other teachers have an important, if under-developed role to play, in supporting students' career planning and awareness through other subjects in the curriculum (Barnes and Andrews, 1995). Personal tutors, too, can exercise considerable influence (Whiteside, 1994), while the tutorial system itself offers a valuable context for tutors and students to work effectively together in the guidance process (Edwards, 1995). There is also an important need to clarify the role of the careers service in the school's overall provision for students (see Section Ten). Recent research findings strongly support the concept of a partnership approach to careers education and guidance, which recognises the respective skills and contributions that can be made by schools, teachers and careers advisers.

There are, however, a number of roles specific to the careers co-ordinator, which need to be discharged effectively if students are to encounter positive experiences of learning in which their own voice can be heard and understood. These are outlined below.

Key Roles

1. Resources and information manager

Students need access to good quality, up-to-date information about the whole range of options that could be available to them, in education, employment and training, and they will need help to develop the information processing skills necessary to make effective use of the data available (see Section Five). If this function is under-developed in schools, it will adversely impact upon whatever careers work happens elsewhere. For example, Hillage and Hirsch (1996, page 7) maintain that:

> *...being able read the market is rapidly becoming an essential skill for anyone seeking to enter or to prosper in the modern labour market.*

While the careers service is a major provider of labour market information, careers co-ordinators occupy an important intermediate position in ensuring that students, parents and colleagues have access to key sources of information and can use it effectively. This role extends beyond managing the careers library. It stresses the importance of creative approaches to information generation and use, and the critical need for students to be proficient in locating, processing and evaluating data for their own planning and decision-making.

2. Co-ordinator of learning opportunities and activities

In *Looking Forward* (1995), SCAA have advocated that students should have an entitlement to an ongoing programme of careers education and guidance, from Year 7 through to Year 13. Most co-ordinators will aim to ensure that such a programme will enable students to develop and use career-related knowledge, skills and understanding in a progressive and coherent manner. This invariably means an important role for the careers co-ordinator in negotiating and planning provision with other internal colleagues and external agencies linked to the school.

Even if the careers co-ordinator is not directly involved in the classroom delivery of careers education, co-ordinating and organising an effective programme of learning remains a key responsibility. Someone needs to be doing the thinking and planning. Resources also need to be won, and training and support for others involved in careers work need to be provided.

3. Interpreter and advocate

If students are to be given sufficient individual help to make sense of educational pathways, training, and employment possibilities, and to prepare effectively for transition, they will need access to careers co-ordinators and careers advisers who are at least 'up with the game'. Careers co-ordinators need to be knowledgeable if they are to be a resource worth using. Yet is good information enough on its own? The 'opportunity structure' for youth employment has changed markedly during the past 15 years or so.

Predicting future employment trends is always problematic. So how well do we expect young adolescents to cope with the risks and uncertainties of new employment trends and transitions?

Do you think Roberts (1996) is right to assume that problems associated with changing 'opportunity structure' and employment trends have become accepted and normalised for young people?

Careers education and guidance has to be an active process, which means in practice individual students having access not only to information, but also to the advocacy skills of a careers co-ordinator or careers adviser willing to act on their behalf in helping them to find suitable opportunities. Many teachers and careers advisers will readily adopt such an approach, but the current pre-occupation of the careers service in meeting the action-planning targets may well militate against this and require careers co-ordinators to reconsider this aspect of their role. Given, too, that careers guidance cannot be separated from the lives that students experience beyond school, closer links with pastoral staff, Education Welfare, Social Services, Housing and other related agencies may become increasingly important when helping students deal with transition, whether into continuing education, employment or a period of uncertainty.

4. Communicator and networker

Careers work is probably the area of the curriculum that involves more contact with external agencies and organisations than any other. Building contacts with employers, colleges, universities and the careers service is just part of the careers co-ordinator's function. Marketing, selling, persuading and negotiating should all be stock-in-trade skills for careers co-ordinators, especially if their remit includes work-experience or similar aspects of the work-related curriculum. Little can be achieved in careers work without the involvement and support of other people. Students need access to 'significant others', from inside school and from the community itself. They need to know who are the 'gatekeepers' into employment and education, how they operate, what they require and how they can be influenced. Law (1991, 1995 page 18) has argued that:

> *the wider and more diverse the range of encounters your students make, the wider and more diverse their ideas will be about the kinds of people they could become ... such thinking implies that your students should meet more people. In particular, it suggests that it is useful to put students into direct and personal contact with people whom they would not otherwise meet.*

Effective networking and liaison with employers and outside agencies suggests a strategic rather than a marginal role for those involved in careers education and guidance. It requires co-ordinators to manage as professionals, rather than as technicians (Boydell, 1985).

Reviewing Your Role in Careers Education and Guidance

The four 'cameo' roles of the careers co-ordinator described above present something of a partial picture, which is intended to aid reflection on how you see your role within your own school context. Part of the argument so far is to suggest that in managing careers education and guidance, co-ordinators need to have a clear sense of their own philosophy and values in careers work, not simply a concern with gaining proficiency in discharging management related tasks and functions – important though these are. Table 8.1 can be used to review your own 'competence' in relation to these roles, and to add any roles of your own which you consider to be of equal or greater importance.

Can you provide 'evidence' or examples of your competence in each of the careers co-ordinators key roles?

Table 8.1 Reviewing competence in the key roles of the careers co-ordinator.

	I feel competent in this role and I am sure that I fulfil it effectively	I am moderately competent in this role but may need to develop it further	I am not very competent in this role and may need to focus on its development
Resource Manager			
Co-ordinator of learning opportunities and activities			
Interpreter and advocate			
Communicator and networker			

© Network Educational Press Ltd, 1997

Managing and Co-ordinating Careers Education and Guidance

Key tasks

We have so far dwelt upon the key roles of the careers co-ordinator, presented especially from a student-centred perspective. But what does a careers co-ordinator do? Having considered some of the basic or key roles, we can begin to identify the tasks and activities that need to be performed in order to function in these roles effectively. Although the job of the careers co-ordinator will be defined differently by each school, there are a number of tasks and responsibilities that need to be carried out by anyone occupying this role, many of which involve a significant range of managerial skills. Some examples are provided below.

1. **Policy and forward planning** requires:

   ● an agreed school policy for careers education and guidance, which includes a statement of student entitlement

   ● a current development plan which rests upon an audit and review of present work, and which identifies areas where good practice can be consolidated or improved and new developments to be undertaken

   ● identification of the resources needed for the development plan's implementation

   ● negotiation of resources and funding to be made available

2. **Administration and organisation** requires:
   - an up-to-date database or record system of all contacts, orders and budgetary information
   - an effective system for recording information for and about students
   - regular reviews and consultation with other key personnel
   - good communications
   - effective meetings

3. **Programme and learning** requires:
   - a clear set of aims and objectives for each stage of the programme
   - schemes of work
   - curriculum guidelines for tutors delivering the programme
   - a policy on the approach to teaching and learning
   - clarity about recording and assessment
   - a system for monitoring, feedback and review

4. **Team development** requires:
   - the enlistment of other colleagues who can and will be committed and make an effective contribution to the careers programme
   - team members who are motivated and valued
   - team members who can give and receive constructive feedback about teaching, student learning and programme development
   - conflict management
   - training opportunities

5. **Liaison with partners** requires:
   - effective relations with the careers service and a service level agreement that is 'enabling' rather than 'constraining' for all concerned
   - clear guidelines for involving and informing parents
   - effective networking with businesses
   - regular contacts with other schools and colleges

6. **Quality, standards and dissemination** requires:
   - agreed standards for all aspects of the programme, which take account of inspection requirements as well as other principles of good practice
   - systems for monitoring and evaluating performance against standards
   - dissemination and promotion of achievements to colleagues within school and 'significant others' in the community

7. **Self-development** requires:
   - an accurate job description based upon a recent job analysis
   - clarity about professional values, goals, strengths and weaknesses
   - time management
   - time for systematic enquiry and reflection
   - feedback and support from 'critical friends' or mentors
   - membership of a professional community of fellow practitioners
   - a vision about 'the best that can be done' for students and others connected with careers education and guidance

Would you suggest any other key tasks for the careers co-ordinator?

A mere list of tasks is of minimal value by itself. However, it is possible to take the components listed under each of the seven headings above and use them as a basis for reviewing or constructing a development plan (Table 8.2).

Table 8.2 Framework for constructing a development plan for careers co-ordinators.

	Examples of where significant progress has already been made	Examples of work in hand, which needs to be either reviewed or completed	Target dates	Examples of new areas of work that need to be developed	Target dates
Policy and forward planning					
Administration and organisation					
Programme and learning					
Team development					
Liaison with partners					
Quality, standards and dissemination					
Self-development					

© *Network Educational Press Ltd, 1997*

Take the framework in Table 8.2, perhaps enlarge it onto an A3 sheet, and complete it as applicable to construct your own development plan.

Developing Self and Role

It is quite feasible to have a clear idea about key roles and tasks and still not be very effective as a co-ordinator. Professional effectiveness can be determined by a wide range of factors, some of which are easier to change and influence than others. Being effective in any role does, however, require an objective level of self-knowledge about those attributes that you already have and those you still need to develop. A brainstorming exercise can help to achieve a greater awareness of the knowledge, skills and qualities that:

- you already possess as both a teacher and co-ordinator/manager, and how these complement or conflict with one another

- you want to develop in relation to your role as co-ordinator

---

Law (1991, page 15) has described a number of functions associated with co-ordinating and managing careers education and guidance, which also contain implicit 'statements' about the potential levels of effectiveness at which co-ordinators can operate. These descriptions could provide the basis for self-assessment and reflection, and contribute useful information towards your own 'personal learning plan' (Table 8.3).

Table 8.3 'Personal learning plan' for careers co-ordinators.

	I am confident about my ability to do this because...	I am not fully confident about my ability to do this and would need to...
Strategic awareness – getting a broader view of how careers work fits into national and local priorities		
Enlistment – finding team members: new people in the school and in the community who can become involved in the school's careers work		
Target-setting – helping people to find what to aim for		
Gaining commitment – helping people to feel good; working with partners so that they value shared work and see it as work they want to do		
Supporting – backing people up and giving them a mandate		
Personnel development – giving training and other forms of staff development; helping partners individually to develop their own sense of direction and their own effectiveness		
Co-ordination – maintaining coherence; knowing what is going on; making sure the right hand knows what the left hand is doing and understanding how each contribution fits into the whole		
Evaluation – identifying the value of everybody's work		
Promotion – establishing the value and worth of your careers work in the eyes of others		
Tactical development – spotting the 'best next action' for you and your partners		

© *Network Educational Press Ltd, 1997, (adapted from the* **Open College's 'Careers Work'**, *Module 8)*

How would you assess your current abilities on the learning plan in Table 8.3?

Another important dimension to effectiveness is the extent to which the co-ordinator is reflective about his/her practice. It can be argued that the reflective manager is the effective manager! Reflection on practice and experience can be further heightened using systematic and straightforward approaches to monitoring and evaluation, which provide a variety of data for informed decision-making and action. Action research provides a useful model for considering how you can become more organised and reflective in developing both your own role and aspects of the careers programme. McNiff, Lomax and Whitehead (1996, page 47) provide a summary of the key stages of the action research cycle (Figure 8.1).

Figure 8.1 Key stages of the action research cycle (after McNiff, Lomax and Whitehead).

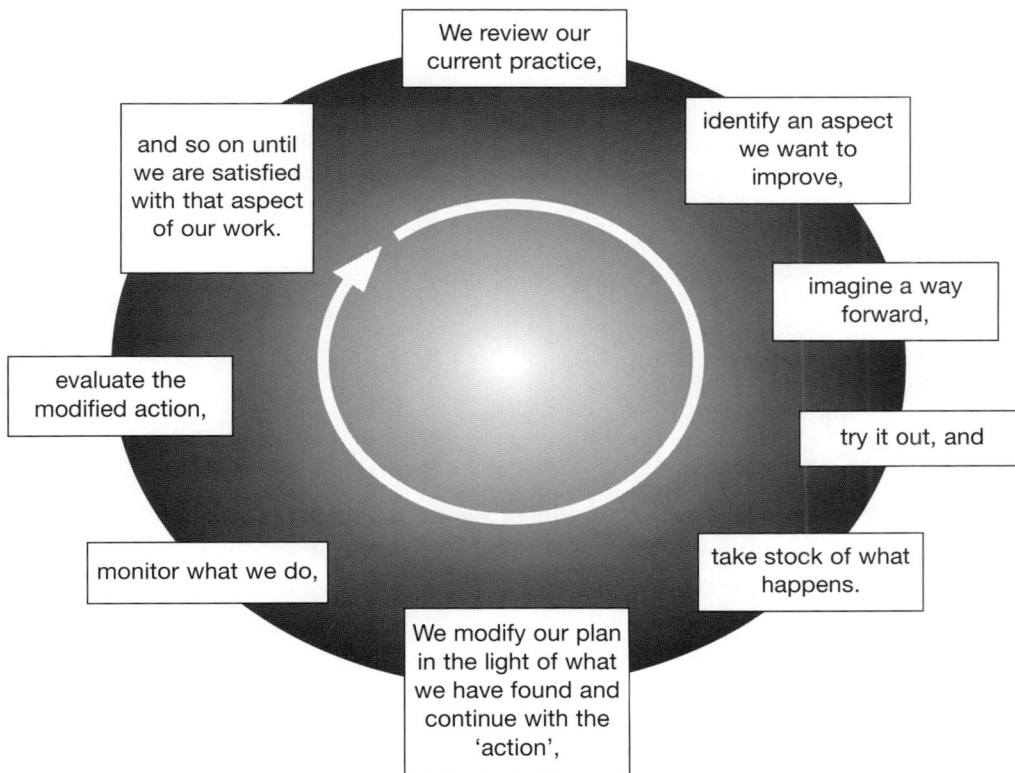

The various models for improving effectiveness offered by action researchers have certain features in common. For example, they encourage professionals to systematically reflect on their experiences, with the intention of consolidating or re-formulating personal (or organisational) understanding about the ubiquitous 'what', 'when', 'why' and 'how' questions.

Self-development likewise requires a capacity to reflect upon and use experiences to change and improve what we do. Self-development needs to be worked on in order to build confidence and overcome any barriers or blockages that may inhibit personal learning and growth. Boydell (1985) argues that the best managers are not necessarily those who have attended numerous courses, but who use their initiative and take every opportunity to increase their knowledge or change their behaviour in order to be more effective with others, for their mutual benefit. He suggests that to be effective, self-development involves:

- taking risks, starting things off, making things happen, explaining your ideas
- reflecting on what has happened
- trying out new ideas, explaining alternatives, finding creative solutions
- listening, being open to ideas, questioning, considering others' ideas and feelings
- planning, thinking ahead
- giving meaning, seeing totality

Being an effective co-ordinator and manager of careers work involves more than simply being a good 'technician manager' – good at carrying out procedures and standard routines. For people who are purely 'task-driven' that may suffice, but students need help in self-development from careers staff who are at the very least, active agents in their own self and role development. Careers co-ordinators can themselves receive support for their own self-development through participation in local associations and meetings, or through membership of the National Association for Careers and Guidance Teachers.

Support could also be generated internally by arranging for a trusted colleague, who is willing to offer you some mentor support, to act as a sounding board for your ideas and to give you some objective feedback. Self-development seldom takes place in isolation. Careers co-ordinators are part of a 'guidance community' of professionals who share many of the same interests and concerns, and who can together articulate a larger vision of good practice. Being able to exchange ideas and experience is an important factor in personal growth and learning.

Action Points

☐ Review the extent to which the careers co-ordinator's role has been adjusted in your school or college to take account of changes in education and training and the youth labour market.

☐ Assess your level of confidence and competence in the four key roles.

☐ Use the seven key management tasks as a basis upon which to construct a development plan for your 'careers department'.

☐ Develop your own personal learning plan.

☐ Consider how the action research cycle can help you to take a more systematic approach to managing and developing your practice.

☐ Identify a colleague who might be prepared to act as a mentor.

Effective Careers Education and Guidance

Managing Staff Development in Careers Work

In Section Nine we learn that:

☞ *The provision of effective staff development is an important strategy for enlisting colleagues' support for careers work.*

☞ *Identifying priorities for staff development requires clarity about the purpose it is intended to serve.*

☞ *There are a variety of 'teaching and learning' methods that can be applied to staff development for careers work.*

☞ *Networks can often provide access to people with the resources and expertise to support your staff development needs.*

☞ *Learning outcomes or performance indicators can provide measures of success.*

☞ *Setting up a staff development episode benefits from prior consultation.*

☞ *Evaluating staff development is important and can be managed simply and effectively.*

The aim of this Section is to consider the benefit that effective staff development can have for teachers involved with careers education and guidance in your school, and to look at some of the principles and methods that underpin successful practice.

We have acknowledged in earlier Sections in this book that many different teachers share a common responsibility for contributing to their students' future planning for learning and work. Some teachers exercise this role more readily than others, either out of necessity, interest, or because they have relevant skills and expertise. Other teachers may prefer to minimise their involvement in careers education and guidance for the very opposite reasons. Yet the inescapable fact remains that the careers co-ordinator alone cannot possibly hope to meet the career learning needs of the entire student body. Other colleagues must be actively involved, and creating opportunities for effective staff development is one strategy that you can use for this purpose.

Gaining colleagues' interest is of key importance; so too is the process of consultation that should precede staff development itself. We shall return to both of these issues in this Section, but perhaps the first issue for you to be clear about, is your own understanding of what constitutes effective staff development and how it can support other staff in the planning and delivery of careers education and guidance.

How would you define the purpose of staff development for careers work? How do you think this will fit with your colleagues' ideas?

Identifying Staff Development Priorities

If you already have a development plan for careers education and guidance, you may have thought about how staff development can serve particular purposes. Forward planning is useful, since it is highly unlikely that sufficient time will be available in a single year to fulfil all your careers staff development needs. In the context of a development plan, therefore, a series of 'training episodes' taking place over a longer time frame is more realistic and achievable. It is also worth asking if there is scope for including 'careers-related elements' within other staff development opportunities offered across the school, especially when these are directed at 'whole-curriculum' issues.

Consider what staff development for careers work has already occurred in your school, the purposes it was designed to serve, and the outcomes you think it achieved. You could enlarge Table 9.1 onto an A3 sheet and use it as part of a reviewing exercise.

Table 9.1 Looking at past staff development episodes in your school.

Staff development 'episode'	What purposes was it designed to serve?	Did it link in to the: ● careers department's development plan? ● school's staff development policy/plan?	What were the perceived outcomes for: ● participants? ● the careers education and guidance programme? ● pupils' learning? ● the organisation?
1.			
2.			
3.			
4.			

© Network Educational Press Ltd, 1997

Determining Purposes of Staff Development

Reflecting upon past experiences can help to identify priorities for future action. As suggested above, staff development for careers work needs to happen for important reasons, which are likely to be connected with your wider aims and objectives for careers work in school – both present and future. Table 9.2 suggests some possible purposes for staff development.

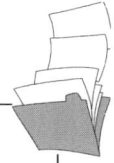

Table 9.2 Staff development purposes.

Some purposes for providing staff development for careers work	Does this apply to your needs and priorities?	What would your staff development need to include to support/develop this aspect of practice?
Helping colleagues to undertake a given task for which they need particular skills and/or knowledge		
Helping colleagues to develop particular roles in supporting careers work		
Helping colleagues to understand the relevance and application of policy and theory to careers work		
Helping colleagues to identify their own concerns about supporting careers work		
Helping colleagues to change their behaviour towards careers work		

© Network Educational Press Ltd, 1997

To what extent does staff development in your school meet the needs of both the individual teacher and the careers programme?

What are the benefits for student learning and for the wider organisation?

Methods of Supporting Staff Development

Effective staff development can be achieved in a wide variety of ways. The methods you choose will be determined by a number of factors, including the underlying purpose(s) you have defined. Your choice will also depend upon whether you intend to use external 'experts' as providers of the training (even if the provision happens in school), or whether you want teachers to negotiate with you first what they want, and how they would like the 'training' delivered. This could still involve an external provider, but the emphasis on negotiation first may suggest that other approaches could be equally appropriate.

Staff development for careers work in school (as opposed to externally accredited courses), usually has to 'compete' for time and resources. An all-day event, hosted at an off-site venue is very attractive, but more typically, smaller slots of half-days, lunchtimes and after-school sessions are the norm. It can be tempting to cram in as much as the time will allow, but it is quite feasible to enrich a short session by providing alternative or additional 'learning opportunities' such as those identified in Table 9.3 by Craft (1996, page 7). This approach allows what can be described as a staff development 'episode', where the learning and application required does not have to rest on a limited, time-bound event, but can be supported over a longer period of time using a variety of resources and approaches. Action research is one such approach to managing staff development, which can result in a more substantial piece of professional learning.

Table 9.3   A range of approaches that can be used in staff development for careers work.

Methods for supporting learning	We do this now Value rating 1-5	This could be a new approach worth using Priority rating 1-5	I need to find out more about this method Priority rating 1-5
action research			
self-directed study			
distance-learning materials			
on-the-job coaching, mentoring or tutoring			
school-based and off-site courses			
job-shadowing or rotation			
membership of a working party or task group			
teacher placement			
personal reflection			
experiential 'assignments'			
collaborative learning			

© Network Educational Press Ltd, 1997

Use Table 9.3 to identify methods for supporting learning that could be integrated into your staff development provision, and allocate value and priority ratings to each.

Identifying Resources and Expertise for Staff Development

Careers co-ordinators are normally active networkers, almost by 'trade'. External contacts are especially valuable since they can provide sources of expertise, or access to resources, which may not be available from within the school. There is no reason why the contribution of professionals from industry or commerce should be limited to the work-experience programme, mock interviews or an industry day. If they bring knowledge, skills or resources relevant to your primary purpose, they are very much in the frame! Identifying the personnel and resources at your disposal could be quite surprising. But do not overlook the school community either, since a number of your colleagues will have experience, expertise and resources that could form an invaluable part of your staff development work. Such colleagues could be used either as consultants or as trainers in their own right.

Table 9.4 Expertise and resources for staff development can be obtained from a range of sources.

School community		Peer community	
People	*Resources*	*People*	*Resources*
● governors	● Business links ● Influence on school's strategic decision making	● other careers co-ordinators	● access to other careers libraries and computer facilities ● collaborative working on joint projects ● sharing resource materials
Business community		**Academic community**	
People	*Resources*	*People*	*Resources*
● Education–Business Partnership	● help for teacher placements ● work-experience award ● mini enterprise	● lecturers ● librarians ● IT specialists	● partnerships for professional development ● academic libraries ● curriculum resource materials ● IT facilities ● conference facilities

Use Table 9.4 in a brainstorming exercise, to identify the full range of resources (human and material) that could be available to your 'careers department'.

Features of Effective Staff Development

One of the key outcomes of an effective episode of staff development will be some form of improved understanding and practice. In order to achieve such outcomes, however, staff must be clear not only about the purpose of the training episode, but also about what will constitute 'success'. In other words, how will we know whether or not the episode has been effective? Our criteria for effectiveness could be defined as either 'outcomes' or 'performance indicators'. HMI (1989) specified a set of indicators that could be used for such a purpose:

- enhanced teacher self-confidence, and readiness to experiment
- changes in the attitudes and behaviours of teachers and pupils
- increased teacher enthusiasm
- raised awareness of the importance of resources
- improved quality of resources used

- greater awareness of new issues and good practice
- new contacts
- new ideas for working in the classroom
- the impact on pupils' learning, motivation, behaviour and attainment

Although this is a set of general performance indicators, they are readily transferable to the careers context and provide a starting point for identifying the particular outcomes you want colleagues to achieve from careers-related staff development.

How could you attempt to measure the criteria listed above, to gauge the success of a staff development episode?

Further research by Joyce and Showers (1988) suggests that staff development can have impact at four different levels:

1. **general awareness** of the new skills
2. **organised knowledge** of the concepts and theory underlying the skills
3. **learning** of principles and skills ready for action
4. **transport and application** of the new skills into the classroom and integration into the teaching repertoire

Moreover, Joyce and Showers contend that the level of impact will depend upon the training method used. Table 9.5 identifies five methods of training that can be used to achieve incremental levels of impact.

Table 9.5　Learning new teaching skills.

Training method or component	Level of impact			
	1. General awareness of new skills	2. Organised knowledge of underlying concepts	3. Learning of new skills	4. Application on-the-job
A. Presentation on, or description of, new skills (e.g. lecture)	✓			
B. Modelling the new skills (e.g. live or video demonstrations)	✓	✓		
C. Practice in simulated settings	✓	✓	✓	
D. Feedback on performance in simulated or real settings	✓	✓	✓	✓
E. Coaching or assistance on-the-job	✓	✓	✓	✓

Setting up a Staff Development Episode

Consultation is an important part of pre-planning for staff development, which can be undertaken either formally or informally. The following example suggests a model for a more formalised meeting, which would take approximately 70 minutes to complete. Such a meeting should prove to be a very worthwhile investment of everyone's time.

Aim of the meeting

The aim is to finalise a brief for the planning group (careers co-ordinator, careers adviser, external adviser) on the desired outcomes for a Year 9 tutors' staff development morning. The training is to be on the tutor's role in monitoring and supporting pupils' option choices.

To be invited
- senior manager
- PSE co-ordinator
- head of Year
- equal opportunities co-ordinator
- a Year 9 tutor
- the careers adviser
- careers co-ordinator
- external adviser/consultant if required

(You will also need to decide who will chair the meeting and who will take notes.)

Process

1. Give the aims of this staff development planning meeting and clarify, if required.
    (5 minutes)

2. **Brainstorm:** list on a flipchart as many ways as possible in which Year 9 tutors currently monitor and support pupils' option choices. Review as necessary.
    (10 minutes)

3. **Discussion:** in order to effectively monitor and support pupils through the options choice process, what do tutors need:
    - in terms of knowledge and understanding?
    - to be able to do?
    (15 minutes)

4. **Discussion:** in the light of this information, what outcomes do we want to achieve from our staff development morning?
    (10 minutes)

5. **Discussion:** what should be the desired level of impact, and which training methods should be used?
    (10 minutes)

6. **Discussion:** what might cause this event to fail? What can we do to counter this?
    (10 minutes)

7. **Summary:** what is the final brief for the staff development planning group?
    (5 minutes)

8. **Review:** the subsequent stages of the planning process.

After the consultation has taken place, you will need to plan for the event or episode in more detail. The **staff development planner** in Table 9.6 attempts to bring together some of the key principles referred to earlier in this Section and should help you think through the issues involved in setting up an episode of staff development.

Table 9.6 Staff development planner.

	Key tasks	Key questions or pointers
1.	Begin by drafting your initial idea. What is the rationale behind it? What purpose is it designed to serve?	Are your ideas based upon past experiences, present and/or future needs? Are your ideas linked to your careers development plan?
2.	Set up a pre-planning meeting and document decisions and outcomes.	Can you use or adapt the model provided earlier in this Section?
3.	Formulate the revised purpose the staff development. The purpose of this event is to:	Try to encapsulate the main purpose of the event into 12–15 words. You will benefit from having a clear focus.
4.	List the specific objectives that you want to achieve:	These objectives may include a range of intended outcomes, which will benefit individual teachers, students' learning, the careers programme and the school as a whole. Framing clear and measurable objectives is preferable since your objectives will become your performance indicators and the basis of your evaluation. Did we achieve what we set out to achieve? How will we know?
5.	Review the time available versus the time needed.	Training often falters because too much was attempted in the time available. Estimate reasonable timings for each element of your programme.
6.	Review the venue and facilities that are desirable with those likely to be available.	Always aim to get the best venue possible, which need not always be the most expensive. If you have to use internal facilities, such as a classroom, prepare the room beforehand, perhaps moving the furniture into a boardroom layout.

Effective Careers Education and Guidance

Table 9.6 Staff development planner (continued).

Key tasks	Key questions or pointers
7. Review the people and resources available.	Identify in the pre-planning stage who you might need and who could be available. The same principle applies to physical resources.
8. Choose method(s) to support learning.	Refer to Tables 9.3 and 9.5. Will this be a one-off event or an ongoing series of linked episodes?
9. Outline your programme.	Ensure a balanced range of activities, linked to the overall purpose of the event.
10. Think about what follow-up work might be required.	How will this be supported? How will progress be monitored?
11. Decide how you will evaluate the session.	Usual methods include short questionnaires, group discussion or individual interviews. What questions do you want to ask? These should be linked to your specific objectives but also include scope to gain feedback on how future sessions could be different.

© Network Educational Press Ltd, 1997

Action Points

☐ Be clear about the definitions that you and your colleagues ascribe to staff development, and about your expectations of it.

☐ Link staff development to a context, such as the careers development plan, school development plan and/or staff development policy.

☐ Be clear about the purposes that you intend staff development to serve.

☐ Review the range of methods available and translate an 'event' into an 'episode'.

☐ Consider the range of expertise and resources that are available from all kinds of sources.

☐ Decide on appropriate outcomes or performance indicators – how will you know when you have achieved what you set out to do?

☐ Consider the relationship between 'impact' levels and training methods.

☐ Undertake pre-planning for a staff development episode.

Section Ten

Schools and Careers Services in Partnership

> **In Section Ten, we learn that:**
>
> ☛ *Partnership agreements are never entirely straightforward, since schools and careers services have different agendas and concerns.*
>
> ☛ *These differences should be recognised but viewed as part of a broader approach to partnership, which helps to overcome suspicion, build trust and improve practice.*
>
> ☛ *NFER findings suggest that the 'guidance community' pattern is the most attractive and effective model of partnership.*
>
> ☛ *Existing practice can be 'audited' against the NFER criteria.*
>
> ☛ *Strategies for developing effective partnerships can be linked to shared projects, which look at improving practice while taking account of the concerns and interests of both parties. Action research is an approach to joint enquiry that is well suited to this purpose.*

The aim of this Section is to explore the present contexts of partnership agreements between schools, colleges and careers services, and to identify what works well and what remains problematic. We shall draw upon recent research evidence, which offers different models for making such partnership arrangements more effective, and illustrate this with reference to two case studies of recent practice.

We shall also look at practical strategies that can be used in problem-solving and confidence-building. Finally, we shall review the critical factors required for partnerships to be fully functioning and effective, and not simply administrative exercises with no bearing on actual practice.

Background to Partnership Agreements

Partnership agreements, usually still described as 'service level agreements' (SLAs), have been in existence in one form or another for many years. Until the Careers Service was taken out of the public sector, each local careers service developed its own approach to negotiating its services with schools and colleges. Approaches varied in their degree of formality, but all were likely to have involved meetings with individual schools to discuss the careers service's role and contribution to the school's careers education and guidance programme. In the past, it was often the careers co-ordinator and the careers adviser who attended such meetings, which were not considered high profile events. Now far more importance is attached to agreements with schools, because so much external funding is attached to each careers service's ability to achieve its 'targets'.

Yet partnership agreements have never been an entirely straightforward process. Schools have sometimes interpreted the exercise as an attempt by the careers service to pursue its own agenda and gain more access to pupils than the school sees as necessary. Careers services, on the other hand, sometimes see the partnership agreement process as too one-sided, focusing on their contribution and eliciting far fewer commitments from schools about their contributions to careers education and guidance.

Today, some schools are more reluctant than ever to allow the careers service to conduct guidance interviews with all Year 11 students, fearing the possible implications for sixth form numbers. Schools and colleges operate within the educational market place and have interests that they wish to protect. It is a strange feature of the present system that a careers service has to 'contract-in' its services, instead of schools and colleges being expected to 'contract-out' careers guidance work to their local careers service. Arguably, this 'market misnomer' undermines the negotiating position of the careers service and goes some way to explaining the difficulties it encounters in establishing open and equal partnership agreements.

Yet students have a statutory right to receive clear and impartial guidance at the appropriate times in their school careers, which the careers service is charged with providing. The important question, therefore, in the context of establishing effective partnerships, is whether the prevailing post 16 issue will continue to dominate negotiations, or whether a much broader notion of partnership can be achieved, which overcomes suspicion and develops mutual trust and professional collaboration.

Reviewing Existing Practice

It is always tempting to dismiss or under-value a process when it can be a source of disagreement as well as agreement. Contracts, in one guise or another, are probably here to stay – the question is how the setting up of contracts can become a gateway to collaboration rather than a barrier to be surmounted. We shall consider some of the insights gained from recent national research on this issue.

You may find it worthwhile to combine information from the research with a SWOT analysis, which can help you to gain a balanced overview of how your present partnership arrangements are working (Figure 10.1). This could be done as a joint exercise, involving both the careers co-ordinator and careers adviser, and provides a useful basis for exploration and discussion.

Brainstorm a list of key points or examples related to each of the headings in Figure 10.1. Try to cite evidence for each example given – this helps to strengthen the value of the exercise, which can be used in both evaluation and future planning.

Figure 10.1   Grid for a SWOT analysis of your current partnership agreements.

Strengths of present partnership	**W**eaknesses of present partnership
Opportunities for improving our partnership	**T**hreats to improving our partnership

© *Network Educational Press Ltd, 1997*

You might want to review your own SWOT analysis after you have considered the findings from a report by NFER researchers Morris, Simkin and Stoney (1995), who investigated the role played by careers services in careers education and guidance in schools. Their findings were drawn from a sample of 66 schools from 11 areas of England and Wales, and revealed three broad models that characterised the ways in which schools and their careers services worked together.

- **Parallel Provision** was characterised by a minimum of interaction between the school and the careers service, and arose when schools attributed low status to careers education and saw the careers service's work as an interruption, rather than an enhancement. In other instances, because the careers services were experiencing staffing difficulties, the schools had become more self-sufficient in providing a comprehensive programme of their own.

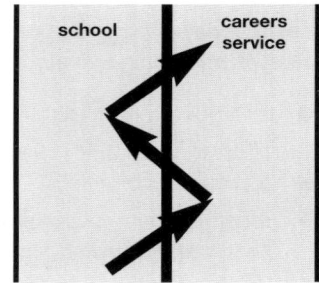

- **Pyramidal Provision** was suggested where schools placed emphasis on the guidance interview with the careers service as the culmination of the preceding careers work within the school. Communications and information exchange tended to work quite well, and this aspect of the careers service's role and contribution was quite well understood and appreciated by a wide range of staff. Careers advisers, however, frequently felt that their contribution could be much enhanced if they were able to contribute to the development of the school's careers education programme, tackling issues arising in interviews much earlier on.   This was the predominant model in the sample investigated, found in around two-thirds of the schools.

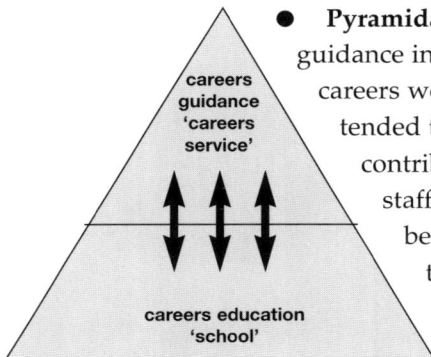

- **The Guidance Community** model required a mutual awareness of individual roles in the school and careers service. The skills of teachers and careers service staff were complementary, and used constructively within the overall design of the school's careers programme. Careers advisers were more actively involved with teachers in team-work, networking, curriculum planning and review. The research indicated that in schools adopting his more 'collaborative' model, students achieved higher levels of careers related skills.

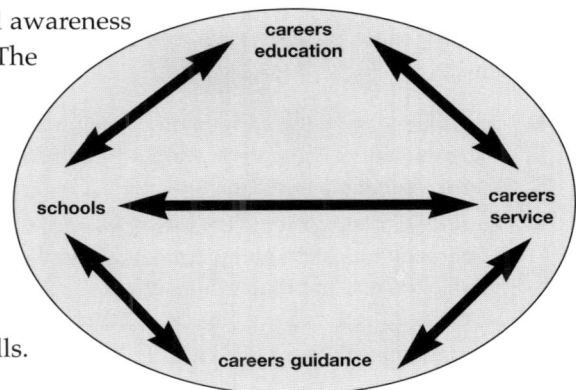

Achieving a 'Guidance Community' Model of Partnership

The guidance community is still an emerging concept, and was found in less than one in six schools surveyed. While there is no blueprint for transforming one type of partnership instantly into another, there are conditions that make one type of model more favourable than another. For example, Morris, Simkin and Stoney (ibid. pages 92–93), suggest that the favourable conditions for a guidance community approach include the factors listed in Table 10.1.

Table 10.1 Favourable conditions for adopting a guidance community approach to partnership with a careers service.

Conditions	This happens at present and examples include...	This doesn't happen at present. What would need to change to bring provision in line with these criteria? Who would need to be involved?
Senior management support from both the school and careers service, in respect of: • appropriate time allocations for the careers adviser to work in the school • a programme of INSET, including shared training • a commitment to careers education and guidance by senior management and other staff • an appointed careers co-ordinator with the necessary skills and resources		
Enabling structures in the school such as: • adequate time allowance for the careers co-ordinator • regular meetings between the careers co-ordinator and careers adviser, and a system for monitoring, evaluating and reviewing the careers programme • a forum that enabled the careers co-ordinator and the careers adviser to meet with senior teaching staff • a mechanism for implementing change • a means whereby members of the wider community can make appropriate contributions to the curriculum		
Mutual awareness of skills, resources and assistance, including: • an awareness by the careers co-ordinator and senior management of the potential input that the careers service can make • an understanding by the careers adviser of the place of careers education and guidance within the school's curriculum and approach to teaching		

© *Network Educational Press Ltd, 1997*

> To what extent is each of the factors described in Table 10.1 present in your school?
>
> Is there scope for action to reduce 'restraining' factors and increase 'enabling' factors, to move your situation progressively towards the guidance community model?

Strategies for Developing Effective Partnerships

Collaboration and common purpose lie at the heart of effective partnerships. To achieve the criteria for effective partnerships identified by the NFER researchers (Table 10.1) practical strategies are required. One careers service and its local college of higher education developed such a strategy, in recent years. It consisted of a series of thematically-based action research projects, set within the context of joint staff development and training, for teachers and careers advisers. Each project lasted for three terms, and provided funding for two or three days of group-work at a course centre and two days of development work in school. The 'contact' days included short presentations by the project tutors, group activities, peer exchange and action-planning. At the end of the project, peer presentations were made on project outcomes, which became part of the review and evaluation process.

The two case studies below illustrate the types of projects that were undertaken and the ways in which respective roles and responsibilities were allocated.

Case Study One

This first case study looks at a collaborative project between the careers co-ordinator from a grammar school and his careers adviser. The project aimed to develop the confidence and skills of Year 9 tutors to deliver a series of lessons on option choices for Year 9 pupils. The careers co-ordinator and careers adviser set about planning the stages of the project as outlined in Table 10.2.

Table 10.2 Planning a project to develop the careers work skills of Year 9 tutors.

Stage of project	People involved
1. Develop action plan following initial meeting, evaluate existing practice, establish aims	careers co-ordinator, careers adviser
2. Design programme, produce materials, develop training procedure, produce programme of activities	careers co-ordinator, careers adviser
3. Meeting with tutors, consult tutors and provide them with materials and other resources	careers co-ordinator, careers adviser, Year 9 tutors
4. Delivery of programme to pupils within five week block of PSE	Year 9 tutors and pupils
5. Evaluation of the programme involving staff and pupils, including a staff assessment of whether the programme had met its objectives	careers co-ordinator, careers adviser, Year 9 tutors, Year 9 pupils

The evaluation provided useful evidence, as much about how to manage staff development as about the curriculum programme itself. For example, the authors noted that:

> *...the approach we used to involve tutors was flawed. We brought them in at a stage when most of the programme and activities were developed so they felt that it was not their programme, but rather an activity that had to be done.*

Nonetheless, throughout the whole process, the careers co-ordinator and careers adviser worked closely together in:

- setting the aims of the project
- designing the project materials
- raising tutors' awareness of the issues and offering practical support
- increasing students' use of the careers library and resources
- working collaboratively in running a staff development session
- working collaboratively on a Year 9 options evening for parents and pupils
- raising the profile of careers education and guidance among tutors, pupils and parents.

On the negative side for the school, the local careers service moved the careers adviser mid-way through the project, which, according to the careers co-ordinator:

> *...has made the evaluation of the project extremely difficult, undermining the momentum developed in terms of tutor and pupil confidence in the careers adviser and the good working practices which have arisen.*

This case study illustrates how nothing ever runs quite to plan. However, a number of the guidance community principles were present in this project and could probably have been developed further, had there been a higher level of consultation earlier in the project, and had the careers adviser not been moved from the school at an untimely moment.

How do you think the principles underlying the guidance community model could have been strengthened in the partnership featured in this case study? Does this example offer any suggestions for your own practice?

Case Study Two

A second project linking a careers service and its local college of higher education involved the teacher in charge of an Extended Education Unit (EEU) at a school for students with severe learning difficulties, and a careers adviser with special responsibilities for students with learning difficulties. Students in the EEU were already involved in the process of action-planning as part of the Youth Award Scheme (Bronze Level), but were finding it a difficult operation. The teacher and careers adviser wanted to use the action research project as a basis for reviewing the existing process of action-planning, with a view to helping students develop their information seeking skills.

Managing the project
The project had several phases of development, as listed below. The careers adviser, teacher in charge and the EEU class teaching team were all involved in both the delivery

and evaluation of each phase. The teacher in charge of the EEU took responsibility for keeping the senior management team informed of the process and the outcomes.

1. Self-assessment activities were developed using written materials supplemented by the use of the *Widgit* software programme, which uses symbols to support written words. These activities were developed collaboratively by the teacher in charge of the EEU and the careers adviser.

2. The local careers service's action plan was adapted using the *Widgit* software and the outcomes of the self-assessment sessions were incorporated. Visitors from the 'world of work' were invited in to talk to the students, to help them ask the right questions and to develop their listening skills. Students were also encouraged to carry out research tasks using the careers library and local library, and by talking to other external visitors.

3. The outcomes of the self-assessment activities and the action plan were recorded in a document that had some 'currency', again utilising the *Widget* software. The outcomes were student CVs, each to be included as part of the student's Record of Achievement.

The evaluation revealed a number of important outcomes for students' learning and confidence. It also drew attention to the 'very close working relationship' between the school staff and the careers adviser, which was described as both 'supportive and positive'.

Can you identify aspects of the guidance community model that are illustrated by this case study?

Does this example offer any suggestions for your own practice?

The action-planning process used throughout the projects in these case studies draws upon some of the basic principles and features of an action research approach to improving professional practice. Emphasis is also placed on the importance and value of reporting findings to an appropriate audience, either within the school, the careers service or the wider community. Even without funding, this is an approach that can be linked to joint staff development activities, or to the work of a forum such as the local careers association, or agreed between the school and the careers service through the service level agreement. The key feature is to identify common issues and concerns that need change and improvement, and to approach the task on a systematic and collaborative basis. Using external facilitators, such as tutors from higher education, can offer a further dimension, but the approach does not depend upon external involvement to become a workable strategy for change.

Thinking About Change

Change remains a prominent and common feature in the relations between schools and their careers services. Change processes are complex since so many variables are at work within both organisations, as well as in the wider environment. Add unplanned factors such as changes in government policy, changes in key personnel and other unforeseen developments, and it soon becomes clear that planning for every eventuality is an impossible task. Partnerships therefore need room to grow and adjust to changing circumstances.

Fullan (1993, pages19–41) argues that there are eight lessons arising from a new paradigm of dynamic change in education, which acknowledge that 'cause and effect' are not close in time and space and that other 'unplanned' factors dynamically interfere and sometimes fail to produce expected outcomes. Fullan's non-linear paradigm suggests a new way of thinking about change processes, which should be viewed as a whole since no one lesson would be useful by itself. This paradigm provides a useful conceptual framework with which to review how schools and careers services deal with the forces of change in the context of their partnership arrangements. Fullan's paradigm has been summarised in Table 10.3 with additional explanatory commentary and key questions to aid schools and careers services in reviewing and developing their own understanding about the partnership relationship. Fullan's approach contains a radical edge.

> **Can you generate your own 'reflective inquiry' by applying Fullan's conceptual framework to your own partnership situation?**

Table 10.3 Fullan's paradigm.

Lesson	Fullan's explanation	Commentary and key questions
Lesson one: You can't mandate what matters (The more complex the change the less you can force it.)	The acid test of productive change is whether individuals and groups develop skills and deep understandings in relation to new solutions. Mandates alter some things, but don't affect what matters. When complex change is involved, people do not and cannot change by being told to do so. Effective change agents neither embrace nor ignore mandates. They use them as catalysts to re-examine what they are doing.	Careers services have been mandated by central government to provide careers guidance in schools. The 1997 Education Act extends that mandate to schools themselves by requiring co-operation with careers services. Externally devised targets limit freedom and flexibility but also help to ensure minimum standards of provision. ● *How can you implement the external mandate while ensuring that the partnership is really able to address what matters in relation to your students' needs for careers education and guidance?* ● *How can the mandate be used to develop the skills, creative thinking and committed action of those involved?*
Lesson two: Change is a journey, not a blueprint (Change is non-linear, loaded with uncertainty and excitement, and sometimes perverse.)	Another reason that you can't mandate what matters, is that you don't know what is going to matter until you are into the journey. If change involved implementing single, well-developed, proven innovations one a time, perhaps it could be blueprinted ... Difficulties are a natural part of any change scenario. And if people do not venture into uncertainty, no significant change will occur.	Partnerships are not based upon situations which are static or which progress in a linear and predictable fashion. Scope for adaptation and new direction is important. ● *Can you be flexible in changing or modifying agreements when the circumstances change, or are they 'written in tablets of stone'?* ● *Partnerships need to be able to grow and evolve. The capacity to learn together as circumstances change is crucial. How can you create such an approach?*
Lesson three: Problems are our friends (Problems are inevitable and you cannot learn without them.)	Problems are endemic in any serious change effort, both within the effort itself and via unplanned intrusions. Problems are necessary for learning, but you also need a capacity for inquiry to learn the right lessons ... In short, problems are your friends, but only if you do something about them.	Fullan cited Louis and Miles (1990) who found that, when confronted with a problem, the least successful schools they studied engaged in 'shallow coping' – doing nothing, procrastinating, doing it the usual way – while more successful schools went deeper to probe underlying reasons and to make substantial interventions. ● *How do you respond to problems when they arise? Do you see them as obstacles to be avoided or as opportunities to learn together?* ● *Fullan argues that a spirit of openness and inquiry is essential to solving problems. How well does this describe your school's approach?*

Effective Careers Education and Guidance

Table 10.3 Fullan's paradigm (continued).

Lesson	Fullan's explanation	Commentary and key questions
Lesson four: Vision and strategic planning come later (Premature visions and planning blind.)	Visions come later for two reasons. First, ... one needs a good deal of reflective experience before one can form a plausible vision. Vision emerges from, more than it precedes, action. Even then it is always provisional. Second, shared vision, which is essential for success, must evolve through the dynamic interaction of organisational members and leaders. Visions die prematurely when they are mere paper products churned out by leadership teams, when they are static or even wrong, and when they attempt to impose a false consensus suppressing rather than enabling personal visions to flourish.	Partnership agreements cannot be negotiated in a vacuum. Schools need to have a sense of their own vision and purpose for careers education and guidance. ● *How would you describe the vision you have for careers education and guidance within your school?* ● *Is it provisional in that it develops on the basis of the reflective experience of yourself and others?* ● *Is the vision shared by others, the result of discussion and agreement between senior managers, the careers co-ordinator and the careers service?* ● *Does the vision inform and shape the partnership agreement?*
Lesson five: Individualism and collectivism must have equal power (There are no one-sided solutions to isolation and group thinking.)	In moving towards greater collaboration we should not lose sight of the 'good side' of individualism. The capacity to think and work independently is essential to educational reform ... Keeping in touch with one's 'inner voice', personal reflection, and the capacity to be alone are essential under conditions of constant change forces ... 'Individualism *and* collegiality' is the critical message.	Managing partnerships is a responsibility that should be shared between influential groups and key individuals. Partnerships need a collegial approach to share decision-making and problem-solving but not at the expense of the creativity and insights of the individuals involved. ● *Does your partnership have boundaries? Are these too tight or too loose?* ● *Are individual skills, creativity and resourcefulness balanced with the need to be democratic? If so, how?* ● *Is there a pressure on individuals to conform to the group thinking of the organisation or can they express and develop their own individual visions?*
Lesson six: Neither centralisation nor decentralisation works (Both top-down and bottom-up strategies are necessary.)	Centralisation errs on the side of over-control, decentralisation errs towards chaos ... The centre and local units need each other. You can't get anywhere by swinging from one dominance to another. What is required is a different two-way relationship of pressure, support and continuous negotiation.	Effective partnerships cannot be achieved merely by management edict and control. Yet too much devolution of decision-making to individuals could be problematic, especially for the careers service. But effective partnerships between schools and their careers services also pre-suppose a constructive dialogue between practitioners and managers within the respective organisations. ● *Does the careers co-ordinator in your school have a two-way relationship with his/her own senior management team based upon continuous negotiation?* ● *Does the careers adviser have a similar internal arrangement?*

Table 10.3 Fullan's paradigm (continued).

Lesson	Fullan's explanation	Commentary and key questions
Lesson seven: Connection with the wider environment is critical for success (The best organisations learn externally as well as internally.)	For teachers and schools to be effective two things have to happen. First, individual moral purpose must be linked to a larger social good. Teachers still need to focus on making a difference with individual students, but they must also work on school-wide change to create the working conditions that will be most effective in helping all students learn. Second, to prosper, organisations must be actively plugged into their environments responding and contributing to the issues of the day.	● *Does your partnership put students' career learning needs in the centre?* ● *Does the partnership look at ways of bringing change to the respective organisations, which will ultimately enhance students' learning?* ● *Are both organisations 'connected' to the wider world, by contributing to change as well as responding to it? How can you support this process?*
Lesson eight: Every person is a change agent (Change is too important to leave to the experts – personal mind set and mastery is the ultimate protection.)	There are two basic reasons why every person working in an enterprise committed to making continuous improvements must be a change agent with a moral purpose. First, ... since no one person can possibly understand the complexities of change in dynamically complex systems, it follows that we cannot leave the responsibility to others. Second, ... the conditions for the new paradigm of change cannot be realised by formal leaders working by themselves. Put differently, each and every teacher has the responsibility to help create an organisation capable of individual and collective inquiry and continuous renewal, or it will not happen.	Each individual does make a difference and partnerships can stand or fall on the basis of individual attitudes, especially towards continuous improvement and to making the relationship more effective and dynamic. ● *How committed are you to being an agent of change? Do you see it as part of your personal and professional responsibility?* ● *If the partnership needs to grow and to change in order to become more effective, it needs the contribution of each key player. No-one can afford to stand on the side-line and leave it to others. Are the key players in your partnership assuming an equal role and responsibility in inquiry and renewal? How can you support this process?*

Action Points

☐ **Review your existing partnership with your careers service, using the SWOT analysis technique. Consider what action is suggested by your findings.**

☐ **Consider which of the three NFER models most closely mirrors practice in your school.**

☐ **Identify the steps that need to be taken in order to develop a guidance community model of careers education and guidance in your school.**

☐ **Examine the two case studies and reflect upon how such strategies could be used in your situation to develop effective partnerships with the careers service.**

☐ **Use Fullan's model for thinking about change forces and how you deal with them in the school–careers service partnership.**

Effective Careers Education and Guidance

Networking and External Partnerships

In Section Eleven, we learn that:

☛ *Active networking at a local and national level is a key part of the careers co-ordinator's role.*

☛ *Students benefit from the contacts made through internal and external networking.*

☛ *The scope of the work-related curriculum can be greatly enhanced through creating or participating in partnerships created through networking.*

☛ *Successful partnerships require good management and organisational skills, and a clear recognition of their value for personal, curriculum and organisational development.*

In Section Eight, we argued that networking is one of the key roles of the careers co-ordinator. Students need access to a wider range of experiences and people than the school can provide by itself (Law, 1981). The careers co-ordinator is singularly well positioned to develop links with individuals and organisations that can make an important contribution, to the work-related curriculum in general, and to careers education and guidance in particular.

One of the aims of this Section is to explore some of the ideas associated with networking as a key activity in careers work. Most careers co-ordinators are involved in networking but may not think about it as such, or may see it as an activity which can benefit from being conducted on a more systematic and purposeful basis. Networking, however, is not an end in itself; it is intended to result in something of tangible benefit in meeting the needs of students and for the broader careers programme. Case studies are provided illustrating how partnerships have been formed between schools and external agencies, which offer students valuable experiences of learning, work and supportive adult relationships.

Networking – Concept and Practice

Networking has become very fashionable in recent years, especially in the context of business and commerce where companies can accrue mutual benefit from collaboration, through professional associations or guilds, or in sharing the costs of research and development, manufacturing, and so on. In careers work, networking has a history of its own, with two main practitioner associations providing professional support and networking opportunities for careers advisers and teachers (see Appendix). Much networking also takes place through careers associations and education–business partnerships (EBPs). Most careers co-ordinators already engage in networking, and although they may not use the term or think consciously about why they do it, they do understand its value. Principally, we can think about networking from three different perspectives, as shown in Table 11.1.

Table 11.1 Perspectives on networking. Networking invites your contribution but it also offers you something in return.

Inputs	the contribution you make to internal and/or external networks – information, expertise or skills that could make a difference to a group's effectiveness
Processes	networks provide opportunities for: ● dialogue ● communicating ideas and concerns ● seeking advice and information ● exploring solutions to problems ● building alliances ● forming partnerships ● influencing action ● negotiating and agreeing change
Outputs	information, advice and support that you gain from participating in a network, or from 'penetrating' other networks for information, ideas and resources the relationships that you form or strengthen as a result of your 'inputs' may be 'deliberate', in the sense that you wanted to achieve a particular outcome, or 'serendipitous' – you gained something beneficial by good fortune

Think about some of your own networking experiences or partnerships in terms of inputs, processes and outputs. Were the outputs 'deliberate' or 'serendipitous'?

Law (1991, 1995) argues that your contacts in the community can become resources for students' learning about work and adult life. The contacts can do this by:

● locating students in new **places**

● engaging students in new **tasks**

● putting students in contact with new **people**

Some student groups entering the labour market require particular help and support – perhaps coaching in the skills and techniques needed to gain a foothold in employment. This might especially apply to the 'bottom' 30 per cent in Hutton's 30/30/40 analysis of the British labour market:

> *There is a bottom 30 per cent of unemployed and economically inactive who are marginalised ... the risk is that poverty will turn into an inability even to subsist, and that marginalisation will change into complete social and economic exclusion ... even those on average incomes and above can become victims of pressures beyond their control. They too can be left partially or completely excluded from their social networks ...*

(Hutton, 1996)

Effective Careers Education and Guidance

The impact of structural change within the labour market poses very real and difficult challenges for careers co-ordinators. Networking cannot promise to resolve these problems, but it can provide a vital source of contacts for students looking to enter and/or progress through the 'market' in education, training and employment, whose own resource-bases may be both limited and partial.

Style of Networking

Effective networking requires the application of a wide range of interpersonal and management skills. It also depends upon attitude. Two approaches seem possible:

1. **passive networking** – we respond to other people's initiatives and research, we wait to be informed rather than find out ourselves

2. **active networking** – we are deliberate in our approach to contributing to, and using, networks to the maximum effect

Figure 11.1 Getting 'wired in' to your networks! Networks can be internal or external, formal or informal, careers-related or multi-professional.

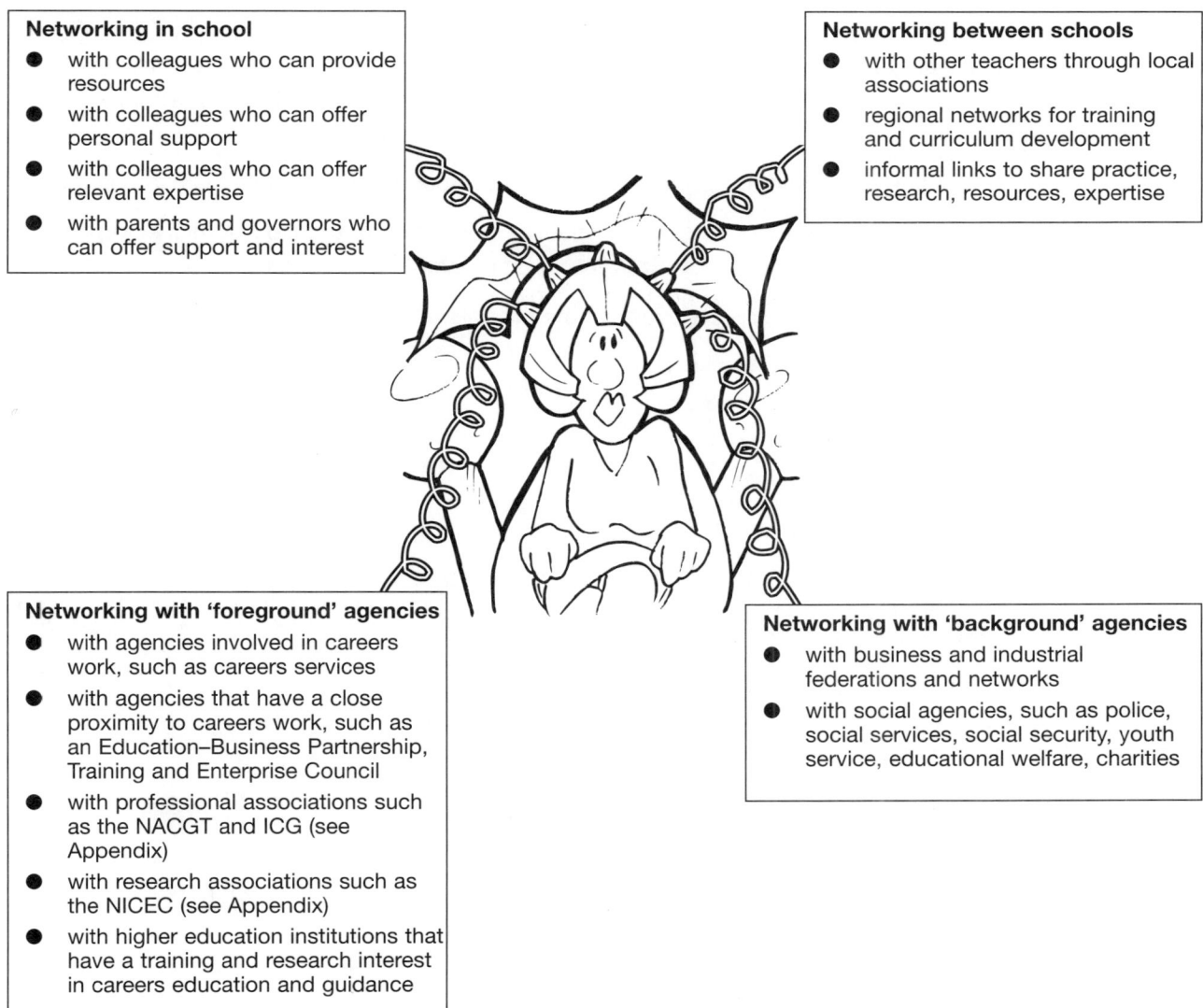

Networking in school
- with colleagues who can provide resources
- with colleagues who can offer personal support
- with colleagues who can offer relevant expertise
- with parents and governors who can offer support and interest

Networking between schools
- with other teachers through local associations
- regional networks for training and curriculum development
- informal links to share practice, research, resources, expertise

Networking with 'foreground' agencies
- with agencies involved in careers work, such as careers services
- with agencies that have a close proximity to careers work, such as an Education–Business Partnership, Training and Enterprise Council
- with professional associations such as the NACGT and ICG (see Appendix)
- with research associations such as the NICEC (see Appendix)
- with higher education institutions that have a training and research interest in careers education and guidance

Networking with 'background' agencies
- with business and industrial federations and networks
- with social agencies, such as police, social services, social security, youth service, educational welfare, charities

External partnerships are only made possible by networking actively with other agencies and individuals. Knowing what networks are open to you is an important first step to forming and extending more effective external partnerships.

Developing External Partnerships

Partnerships with external agencies can serve a number of purposes and contain a particular focus. In some cases this focus can be pre-determined, by participating in an existing scheme organised by an external agency, such as an Education–Business Partnership (EBP). In other instances, you will need to determine the focus for yourself. The examples given in Table 11.2 illustrate fairly typical clusters, but the categories are by no means watertight. Invariably, such partnership arrangements bring different opportunities, demands and benefits, some expected, others unanticipated.

Table 11.2 Examples of focuses for partnerships.

Student focus	including work-experience, work-shadowing, mock interviews, visits, mentoring schemes
Transition focus	providing students with cross-phase experiences, such as 'taster days' in a further education college
Employment focus	such as compact agreements between groups of employers and schools providing opportunities for students
Science and technology focus	such as Neighbourhood Engineers, Crest Awards
Enterprise focus	including events like industry days, mini enterprise, Young Enterprise
Management focus	where schools attempt to learn more about management from an industrial and commercial perspective
Teacher focus	such as teacher placements into industry

Two very different examples of partnership arrangements are provided in the following case studies, involving students, schools, colleges, EBPs, businesses and other important agencies. Each has a different focus but both bring real benefits to students and staff. (Qualifying and quantifying this in league table terms, however, is no simple matter and has to be an issue for further research.)

Effective Careers Education and Guidance

Project title
Tower Hamlets Education–Business Partnership – Business Mentoring Scheme

Background to the project (*aims, profile of participants*)
There are many young people in Tower Hamlets in London who are disadvantaged by their low level of access to skilled job opportunities, due to poverty, unemployment and poor housing. In addition, they lack established networks in the worlds of industry, commerce or the professions. The mentoring project provides young people with access to the wider world of work, and helps to raise opportunity awareness. Mentors are an additional resource to students, providing guidance on working life and further education. The mentoring scheme also provides students with regular individual attention that would otherwise be difficult to obtain in a normal school environment. The purposes of the mentoring sessions are:

- to raise students' understanding of business and industry
- for the mentor to act as a role model
- to improve motivation and raise students' aspirations
- to raise students' self-confidence

The overall aim of the project is to:

- increase understanding between business and education
- improve students' understanding and awareness of business, raise their self-belief and motivation, and enable them to compete more effectively in adult and working life
- offer a valuable form of experience to men and women in business

The scheme, which is sponsored by Lloyds of London, was launched in March 1993 and currently involves students from 14 schools and 99 mentors from industry and commerce.

Each mentor is matched to 4 or 5 students, and works with them as a group. Mentoring with students from special schools takes place on a one-to-one basis.

Methodology of scheme evaluation
The students and mentors were split into eight groups, each of which was set a separate question about the scheme. Both students and mentors then asked three other people the question they had been given and noted down their responses. Each question and response was analysed in turn.

Outcomes (*findings from the most recent annual review*)

Question: What three things do you like most about mentoring?

The three main responses to this question, from the students' perspective, were as follows:

1. mentoring provides an opportunity to meet new people

2. mentoring makes students feel more confident about themselves

3. mentoring gives students a better understanding of the world of work, and helps them attain the skills that are required

Mentors recorded that:

1. mentoring is a great challenge, which gives a valuable insight into education today

2. mentoring prepares young people for the future by providing an outlook on the outside world, with visits to the mentor's workplace making sessions more realistic

3. it is rewarding to see students' skills develop through their mentor's encouragement, especially communication skills

A difficult balance needs to be maintained regarding the time mentors spend with their students, especially due to the requirements of the National Curriculum. Mentors also need to be able to limit the time they spend away from the workplace: there is a danger that the commitment required could become too onerous.

Findings from a school for boys with educational and behavioural difficulties, indicated a marked improvement in concentration and motivation, with raised levels of self-esteem. More broadly, students suggested that:

- the interaction with people they did not previously know, and in particular with different types of people to themselves, greatly helped raise their confidence and improve their communication

- the exercises used in the mentoring sessions helped with interview practice, communication, body language, eye contact and telephone skills

The mentors not only helped to raise students' confidence in actually approaching an employer for a job, but also helped rid them of their nerves when faced with an interview.

Is there a mentoring scheme running at your school already? Does the case study above suggest any ways in which your scheme could be improved or developed?

If you were setting up a new scheme, how would you go about identifying and approaching suitable mentors?

Effective Careers Education and Guidance

Project title
School Time Enterprise Programme (STEP)

Background to the project (aims, profile of participants)
STEP is an inter-agency approach aimed at tackling truancy and helping disaffected young people who might otherwise end up on the fast track to a criminal career. The project aims to reduce truancy by offering recommended students the chance to attend a work-experience placement for one day a week in the last year of schooling. In return, the students must attend full time schooling for the remaining four days.

The project was launched with one school in September 1995. Currently, three schools from North West Kent and the Medway towns are now involved in the project. Each school is asked to establish its own steering group to oversee the selection and placement of students. The steering group includes the school's link teacher, education welfare officer, careers co-ordinator and a police officer from the Constabulary's Inter-Agency Department. A member of the County Council's Youth and Community Department acts as the overall project co-ordinator and liaises with each school's link teacher on the selection of students and the identification of suitable work-experience placements.

A subsequent meeting is held between the steering group, student, his/her parents or guardians and a potential employer. Once a placement has been confirmed, the student and his/her parents are invited to enter into a written agreement between the student, parents and school. Placements are intended to run for a full year but finish in the summer term before examinations start.

Methodology of scheme evaluation
Individual case study reports from each of the three schools were collected and analysed.

Outcomes (products, findings, recommendations)

School One (completed two full terms)
After two full terms had been completed, two students had been withdrawn from the scheme due to lack of interest and motivation. Of the seven remaining:

- all had maintained a 100% school attendance record
- all had maintained a 100% STEP attendance
- none had been in trouble with the police since starting STEP
- six of the group received part-time employment as a direct consequence of the STEP programme
- all showed an improvement in school work and a reduction in disruptive behaviour

School Two (completed one full term)

Five students participated in the scheme. After one term:

- all five had a 100% school attendance rate
- all five had a 100% STEP attendance
- none had been in trouble with the police since starting STEP
- two students received part-time work as a direct consequence of the STEP programme
- all showed an improvement in school work and a reduction in disruptive behaviour

School Three (completed one full term)

A similar pattern emerges for the third school, which placed three students on the scheme, all of whom were still participating by the end of the first term.

The evaluation also highlighted the need for:

- complete and full ownership of the project by individual schools
- commitment by the local police
- commitment by other key agencies
- an effective mentoring scheme – the first attempt to launch a mentoring scheme run by senior managers from within school had not been successful

What implications might a scheme like STEP have for timetabling in your school? How would you overcome any problems?

The partnerships described in this Section link careers co-ordinators into the much broader work-related curriculum, which is largely an inevitable consequence of linking with employers, Education–Business Partnerships and other community agencies. In these partnerships, careers co-ordinators have an important role to play, sometimes in a central position, at other times as part of a larger team of professionals who are pooling their expertise and resources to create worthwhile learning experiences for students. This emphasises the importance of other people in the career learning and development of your students, and that by networking to combine resources, far more can be achieved than by any individual school or agency operating in isolation.

Action Points

☐ Think about how you approach networking tasks by using the inputs, processes and outputs model (Table 11.1).

☐ Consider how active networking will bring benefits to your students.

☐ Map the range of people and agencies with whom you could network. Review the types of partnerships that suit the needs of your particular school.

☐ Consider the value of the two case studies for your own approach to networking and partnerships.

Effective Careers Education and Guidance

Section Twelve

Ensuring Quality

> **In Section Twelve, we learn that:**
>
> ☛ **Evaluation, quality assurance and inspection are three ways of ensuring quality in careers education and guidance.**
>
> ☛ **Evaluation is a formal activity, which benefits from systematic planning.**
>
> ☛ **Schools need to use an OFSTED inspection to meet their needs.**
>
> ☛ **Schools need to weigh up the pros and cons before using local quality standards to develop their careers work.**

This Section aims to help you to improve careers education and guidance in your school as part of a continuing drive to ensure the highest quality of provision for your students. It argues the need for a systematic approach to managing the issue of quality in careers work, and then discusses how to get the most out of three main types of activities to ensure quality: evaluation, quality assurance and inspection.

The Need for a Systematic Approach

A systematic approach to ensuring quality in careers work is essential. Ensuring quality can be time-consuming and complex, and resources in schools are limited, so those involved in monitoring quality must be convinced that the return on their efforts is worthwhile. Table 12.1 describes activities that constitute a practical approach to ensuring quality.

Table 12.1 Ensuring quality.

Activity	Frequency	Potential benefits	Potential limitations
co-ordinator reports to senior managers and governors on the careers education and guidance programme	annual	• provides a comprehensive overview of year's activities • supports reviewing and feeds into school development planning processes	• may be too descriptive
maintaining service level or partnership agreement with the careers service	annual with termly or mid-year reviews	• supports on-going monitoring of activities in the programme • ensures optimal use of expertise and resources available in the school and the careers service	• may be overlooked as a means of developing creative and innovatory approaches to practice
monitoring, review and evaluation of specific activities	regular, in response to needs and priorities, possibly on a rolling basis	• enables checks to be made on the worth or value of specific activities in the programme • allows attention to be focused on agreed needs and priorities where change or improvement is sought • aids decision-making • encourages the selection and use of formal techniques for assessing quality • likely to involve the main stakeholders in any scheme to ensure quality e.g. students, parents	• likely to be time-consuming
inspection	according to the OFSTED cycle	• provides an external check on the strengths and weaknesses of overall provision • may provide a useful basis for future action and improvement	• may not be sufficiently focused on the school's current needs and priorities or be detailed enough
gaining an award for achieving local quality standards	according to the requirements of the scheme, typically renewable every three years	• gives public recognition • provides school with an external check that it is meeting locally agreed standards • adds value where working towards local standards can be integrated with internal review and development processes, and staff development	• a standardised scheme may not meet the school's need to focus on particular aspects to improve quality

Effective Careers Education and Guidance

Getting the Most from Evaluation

The need for evaluation can arise in any area of careers work (Table 12.2).

Table 12.2   Evaluation in different areas of careers work.

Area	Questions that evaluation should address
careers education	● Are students making progress? ● What are the outcomes for students? ● Are students satisfied with the programme?
careers guidance	● How are students benefiting? ● How should careers guidance best be organised?
careers information	● Do students have access? ● Is careers information well used? ● How good are the resources used?
experiences of work	● What benefits do students gain from work-experience? ● How well is work-experience integrated into the careers programme?

Evaluation in this context is the systematic study of the value or worth of an aspect of careers education and guidance provision. The impact of evaluation on quality may be linked to its role in managing careers work. Purposeful evaluation is undertaken to inform and influence decision-makers.

Sometimes schools may participate in large-scale and external evaluation studies. This Section looks at small-scale and manageable evaluation projects, which should be part of the routine activity of all careers co-ordinators.

A step-by-step approach will help you to manage an effective evaluation exercise.

1. Clarify the Scope and Purpose of the Evaluation

Make sure that you are clear about what it is that you wish to find out. Most evaluation activities are prompted by curiosity, uncertainty or concern. A school might pose questions, for example, about the impact on students' learning of a well-established work-experience scheme or module of careers work that has not been reviewed for sometime. It helps if you can frame your evaluation enquiry as a question or series of linked questions e.g. How are students making use of the careers information available in the school? Can we improve on this? If so, how?

What areas of uncertainty or concern in your careers programme do you think might require prompt evaluation? How would you frame your enquiry – what questions would you ask?

Satisfy yourself that this is the most worthwhile evaluation that could be carried out at this time. Sometimes, the demand for evaluation has not been properly considered or has come from outside. Pressure for evaluation comes from two, often competing, sources:

- **accountability** – e.g. demonstrating value for money and the efficient use of resources

- **development** – e.g. encouraging change and improvement

You may be interested in replicating an existing study for your own purposes, but care is needed here. An off-the-peg questionnaire or interview schedule may lead you to ask for information that you do not intend to use. Tampering with an evaluation instrument may lead to unforeseen problems.

2. Plan a Strategy for Communicating and Reporting the Evaluation

The communication and reporting of your findings needs to be considered earlier in your evaluation planning than you might expect. For the findings and recommendations to have maximum impact, you need to have a clear concept of the audience for the evaluation report and in what form it should be presented. Sometimes there is more than one audience and you need to prepare different versions of the report, such as an executive summary and a full report. You need to gain support for the evaluation from those who will be affected, perhaps because it is their work that is the subject of the report, or because they will have played a part in collecting data. Consider how the outcomes of the evaluation will be reported to them. The timing of the presentation of a report can also be crucial – a Thursday afternoon before the end of term is likely to be unhelpful.

3. Formulate your Hypotheses in Relation to the Evaluation Question(s)

Formulating hypotheses helps you to identify the issues you wish to investigate. You may feel, for example, that students are confusing 'enjoyment' with 'learning' in the tutor-delivered careers programme. Some students (and tutors) like to be entertained and prefer something that is not too demanding of them! Perhaps, they do not realise how much more value they could get from the tutor-based careers programme. It is possible to devise a questionnaire or interview schedule to find out what students are getting from tutorial sessions. This may expose wide differences in the performances of individual tutors, which is a sensitive issue requiring careful handling at the outset; but if your evaluation reveals what is happening, you could challenge some very important student myths such as *'our tutor is nice because he just lets us talk'*.

4. Review Existing Literature on the Subject

A review of existing literature will help you to refine your own investigation and put it into context. It is important to know about the ideas and explanations that have already been advanced on the topic of your evaluation.

The results of research and surveys are often summarised in journals such as *Newscheck, Careers Education and Guidance* (published by the National Association of Careers and Guidance Teachers), *Careers Guidance Today* (published by the Institute for Careers Guidance), *The Times Educational Supplement* and in the national press. Research reports are published by the Quality Assurance and Development Unit of the Choice and Careers Division of the DfEE and in journals such as *The British Journal of Guidance and Counselling.*

5. Select an Evaluation Design

Designing an evaluation study involves agreeing a time frame, working out who will be involved, choosing appropriate methods of data collection, and checking the costs. There are two main types of evaluation design:

- **qualitative evaluation** – used for the analysis and interpretation of personal and subjective information which cannot be fitted into standardised categories e.g. students' perceptions of the value of the careers education and guidance programme
- **quantitative evaluation** – used for the analysis and interpretation of information that is numerical and can be categorised and compared statistically e.g. students' use of the careers library

There are various methods of data collection, which each have strengths and weaknesses related to their suitability for your purpose. The main methods are compared in Table 12.3.

Table 12.3 Methods of data collection.

Method	Advantages	Disadvantages
questionnaires	● easy to administer ● easy to process ● can cover a large sample	● foolproof questionnaire difficult to produce ● no opportunity to ask supplementary questions
interviews (one-to-one or group; structured, semi-structured or unstructured)	● yield rich data ● can clarify points raised by the interviewee as they arise	● can take a long time ● analysis of data can become complex ● can be more difficult when the interviewer is known to the interviewee
observation (participant or non-participant; overt or covert)	● represents events and behaviour accurately ● does not depend on explanation by respondents	● complex events and behaviour can be difficult to record ● presence of observer can influence behaviour of group
documents (existing or specially created)	● provide background and contextual information	● may not cover all the information needed

Further advice and information on data collection and analysis is available in general works on educational evaluation. Such works deal with other important issues, including the need to:

- pilot your data collection method
- use an appropriate sampling technique, if necessary
- assess the quality of your evidence e.g. collecting data from more than one source on a particular issue is a technique known as triangulation
- be able to demonstrate that your evaluation is both valid and reliable. Validity is about whether or not the method you use measures what it is intended to measure. Reliability is about whether or not another individual applying your methods would reach the same conclusions.

6. Identify How to Analyse and Interpret your Data

When considering how to analyse and interpret your data, you will need to think about practical matters such as the availability and accessibility of IT to speed up processing, as well as conceptual and technical issues. Important analysis and interpretation techniques include those described below.

Statistical analysis

Depending on the nature of your evaluation study, you can use appropriate techniques such as working out percentages and totals, which can be presented in various ways e.g. bar chart to show students' choices of work-experience placements by gender and occupational groupings; pie graph to show pattern of first destinations of leavers. More complex statistical techniques can be used, if required.

Developing categories

Some types of evaluation enable you to code data under headings which are either based on your existing understanding or which are created as you work through the data. For example, you could evaluate the contribution of tutors to careers education and guidance by developing headings which cover the full range of actions in which they could be involved.

Categories for evaluating the tutors' contribution to careers education and guidance:

- delivery of careers elements of taught tutorial programme
- individual help and support to students
- contribution to home–school links in careers work
- carrying out administrative tasks linked to the careers programme
- working with and through the careers 'specialists' in the school

You need to be able to justify the selection of categories since it inevitably involves judging that some items of data are more important and relevant than others.

Interpretation involves commenting creatively on significant features, trends and patterns in a way that can be reasonably supported by your analysis of the data.

7. Present Your Findings

As discussed above, the way an evaluation report is presented is crucial to its reception by those who are expected to act on its findings.

8. Review the Evaluation Process

Inevitably, in any evaluation study, there are things that you would do differently if you were starting out again. Find time to reflect on what you have learned from doing the evaluation and check that you are getting the most out of it in terms of improving the effectiveness of the careers programme.

Getting the Most from Inspection

To suggest that you might enjoy an inspection of your school's careers work is perhaps going too far. However, preparing for an inspection can be very rewarding – especially if it prompts you to do all those things that you have been meaning to get round to for months! It can also be satisfying to submit your programme to the judgement of an expert professional and to receive public recognition of your school's achievements.

The current arrangements for inspecting careers work by the Office for Standards in Education (OFSTED) still do not go far enough to ensure that inspection is in most cases a worthwhile experience for careers co-ordinators. It can be hit-and-miss whether or not inspection teams pay sufficient attention to the careers provision and whether or not they have an inspector with sufficient expertise to make incisive judgements on strengths, weaknesses and key areas for action.

In the 1995 revision to the Framework for Inspection, the arrangements for inspecting careers education and guidance were strengthened. It is significant that careers education and guidance is identified in the Framework as an area of provision that can contribute to the overall quality and standards of education achieved by schools. In the section on 'Curriculum and Assessment' in the final report, inspectors are required to:

> *...evaluate and report on strengths and weaknesses in ... careers education and guidance in schools providing for the secondary age range.*

The guidance in this section goes on to say that judgements should be based on the extent to which the curriculum:

> *...includes, for pupils of secondary age, careers education and impartial guidance, drawing on the careers service.*

OFSTED emphasises the importance of having a planned and co-ordinated programme of careers education which is enhanced by links with employers. It also stresses the need to provide systematic and impartial careers guidance, drawing on the expertise of outside agencies, particularly the careers service. The overall programme should challenge stereotyping; and inspectors should check that staff involved in careers education and guidance have access to appropriate professional development.

It is helpful for the status of careers education and guidance that OFSTED view it as an aspect of the curriculum and not simply as part of the arrangements for 'support, guidance and pupils' welfare'. In practice though, inspectors have limited time to inspect the school's careers work. Table 12.4 suggests how a 'lead inspector' for careers education and guidance might plan and carry out an inspection.

Table 12.4 How a 'lead inspector' might plan and carry out an inspection.

Before the inspection	• check documentation that has been made available e.g. policy statement, partnership/service level agreement, curriculum guidelines
	• review evidence from TEC, local employers
	• review evidence from parents e.g. at the parents' meeting
	• prepare pre-inspection commentary and identify issues for inspection
During the inspection	• review additional information provided e.g. lesson plans, teachers' records, pupils' work (including action plans and Records of Achievement)
	• organise observations, with support of colleagues where appropriate, e.g. careers lessons, careers library, assemblies, tutor periods, careers interviews, work-experience visits, parents' evenings
	• organise interviews, with support of colleagues where appropriate, e.g. careers co-ordinator, group(s) of pupils, link careers adviser
	• collate and assess quality of evidence; make corporate judgements about quality of careers education and guidance and its contribution to educational standards achieved; complete grade on school judgement recording form
	• give feedback to careers co-ordinator with a senior manager present
	• return documents on loan from the school and thank them
After the inspection	• complete OFSTED documentation, including writing of a paragraph (c.300 words) for 'Curriculum and Assessment' section of final report

Highlight the actions in Table 12.4 that would enable you to show off the best features of your careers provision and help you to make improvements.

What kind of evidence gathering and feedback would be most helpful to your school? Prior to your inspection, try to negotiate this kind of evidence gathering and feedback, through your headteacher.

(Remember that the inspection team visiting your school may not be planning to inspect careers work as suggested in Table 12.4.)

Getting the Most from Local Quality Standards

Many areas are developing or using local quality standards to ensure quality in careers work. Quality focuses on processes and outcomes that are reliable and appropriate. The standards that are applied indicate whether the careers provision is of the highest quality, the minimum acceptable or somewhere in between. Students' needs should underpin any scheme for quality standards. Parents, schools, careers services, employers and others who have a legitimate interest in the quality of provision must be regarded as secondary stakeholders.

The impetus for the burgeoning interest in local quality standards comes from several sources including the wider quality assurance movement. In part, they represent a desire from Training Enterprise Councils (TECs), Local Education Authorities (LEAs), careers services and schools to demonstrate that they are giving value for money for the additional public funds now available. Quality standards also underpin the idea of students' entitlement to careers education and guidance. Undoubtedly, their development reflects a drive to raise standards and to promote recognition of the importance of careers education and guidance.

At the national level, there have been two significant developments to promote good practice in local schemes and greater consistency between them. The first is a publication in the *Better Choices* series on *Quality in Careers Education and Guidance* (DfEE, 1996) setting out criteria for evaluating local arrangements for setting standards and securing quality in careers education and guidance. The second is work being undertaken by the National Advisory Council for Careers Education and Guidance to identify the principles that underpin quality in careers education and guidance.

Worthy as these aims are, they are not sufficient on their own to persuade schools, and in particular careers co-ordinators, to seek recognition through a local scheme. Each school needs to weigh up the merits and demerits of using a local quality standards framework or entering for a local award as a means of improving the quality of careers work. Key points for the careers co-ordinator to consider include those listed below.

- Does the scheme really identify what is involved in securing quality in careers work?
- Is the scheme cost effective? (How much time and effort on your part will the scheme require; and could that time be better spent in other directions?)
- Is the local scheme flexible enough to fit in with your school's own self-review and evaluation processes?
- Can the evidence collected for an award count towards any other scheme that your school is pursuing e.g. Investors in People?
- Will working towards an award help you to do work that you wanted to do anyway e.g. prepare for an OFSTED inspection?
- Are the incentives attractive enough e.g. additional funding for training and development linked to achieving the award?
- Will gaining an award be understood and valued by students, parents and local businesses?

Action Points

☐ Agree your evaluation priorities and incorporate them in your careers education and guidance development plan for the school.

☐ Prepare long term plans for taking an **OFSTED** inspection in your stride.

☐ Devise a strategy for managing quality in careers work, which is manageable and sustainable, and which is consistent with the school's overall approach to managing quality.

Appendix

Helpful Organisations

Birmingham Careers Service
11 Soho Road, Handsworth, Birmingham, B21 9SN   0121 248 8000

Independent Schools Careers Organisation (ISCO)
12A Princess Way, Camberley, Surrey, GU15 3SP   01276 21188

Institute of Careers Guidance (ICG)
27a Lower Higher Street, Stourbridge, West Midlands, DX8 1PA   01384 376464

National Association of Careers and Guidance Teachers (NACGT)
Membership Secretary, 46 Fairfield Road, Penarth,
Vale of Glamorgan, CF64 2SL   01222 702332

National Institute for Careers Education and Counselling (NICEC)
Sheraton House, Castle Park, Cambridge, CB3 OAX   01223 460277

The Trident Trust
Saffron Court, 14b St Cross Street, London, EC1N 8XA   0171 242 1616

The Youth Award Scheme
ASDAN Central Office, 27 Redland Hill, Bristol, BS6 6UX   0117 923 9843

Young Enterprise
Ewert Place, Summertown, Oxford, OX2 7BZ   01865 311180

Bibliography and Further Reading

Ali L. and Graham B. (1996), *The Counselling Approach to Careers Guidance*, Routledge, London

Andrews D., Barnes A. and Law B. (1995), *Staff Development for Careers Work*, NICEC Project Report, Careers Research and Advisory Centre (CRAC), Cambridge

Ball B. (1984), *Careers Counselling in Practice*, Falmer Press, London

Barnes A. (1995), *Quality and Standards in Careers Work* in Frost D., Edwards A. and Reynolds H. (eds), *Careers Education and Guidance*, Kogan Page, London

Barnes A. (ed)(1996), *Managing Careers Work*, Careers Enterprise Group

Barnes A. and Andrews D. (1995), *Developing Careers Education and Guidance in the Curriculum*, Fulton Press

Barnes A., Edwards A. and Nix C. (eds)(1996), *Career Planning Guides*, Careers Enterprise Group

Bell J. (1979), *Doing your research project: a guide for first-time researchers in education and social science*, Open University Press, Milton Keynes

Biggs J. and Moore P. (1993), *The Process of Learning*, Prentice Hall, New York

Boydell T. (1985), *The Management of Self-Development: a guide for managers, organisations and institutions*, ILO, Geneva

Career Choice Education (1991), *Curriculum Guide*, Government of Quebec

Cleaton D. (1993), *Careers Education and Guidance in British Schools*, ICG/NACGT

COIC (1991), *Co-ordinating Careers Work*, COIC, Sheffield

COIC (1992), *Evaluating Your Careers Work*, COIC, Sheffield

Collin A., *Changes in the Concept of 'Career'*, NICEC Careers Education and Guidance Bulletin (Number 46, Summer 1996)

Craft A. (1996), *Continuing Professional Development: A Practical Guide for Teachers and Schools*, The Open University, Milton Keynes, and Routledge, London

Culley, S. (1991), *Integrative Counselling Skills in Action*, Sage, London

Department for Education and Employment (1995), *Better Choices: Putting the Principles into Practice*, DfEE, London

Department for Education and Employment (1996), *Better Choices: Effective Action Planning*, DfEE, London

Department for Education and Employment (1996), *Better Choices: Quality in Careers Education and Guidance*, DfEE, London

Department for Education and Employment (1996), *LMI Matters! A toolkit for people who give advice and guidance on education and employment*, DfEE, London

Department for Education and Employment (1996), *The Report on Effective Teaching and Learning in Work Related Contexts*, DfEE, London

Department for Education and Employment (1997), *Innovative Technology in Careers Guidance*, NEC Conference Report 18/19th March 1997

Duignan P.A., *Reflective management: the key to quality leadership* (1988), in Riches C. and Morgan C. (eds)(1989), *Human Resource Management*, Open University Press, Milton Keynes

Edwards A. (1995), *Post 16 Careers Guidance: The Role of Tutorial Methods in Supporting Good Practice*, in Frost D., Edwards A. and Reynolds H. (1995), *Careers Education and Guidance: Developing Professional Practice*, Kogan Page, London.

Edwards A. (ed)(1994), *Career Guides*, Network Educational Press Ltd. and Kent County Council

Egan G. (1994), *The Skilled Helper*, Fifth Edition, Brooks/Cole Publishing Company, California

Elliot J. (1996), *Paper to the Canterbury Action Research Conference, 4 May 1996*

Fox K. (1995), *Media Education and Careers Education and Guidance (or, I once saw a happy episode of Eastenders)* in Frost D., Edwards A. and Reynolds H. (eds), *Careers Education and Guidance: Developing Professional Practice*, Kogan Page, London

Fredrickson R. H. (1982), *Careers Information*, Prentice Hall, New Jersey Inc.

Frost D. (1995), *Improving Professional Practice through Evaluation* in Frost D., Edwards A. and Reynolds H. (eds), *Careers Education and Guidance: Developing Professional Practice*, Kogan Page, London

Fullan M. (1987), *Managing Curriculum Change* in Preedy M. (ed), *Approaches to Curriculum Management*, Open University Press, Milton Keynes

Fullan M. (1993), *Change Forces, Probing the Depths of Educational Reform*, The Falmer Press, London

Gardner H. (1983), *Frames of Mind*, Basic Books, New York

Grubb N. (1996), *Seminar for NICEC members at the University of London*, Institute of Education, 24th September 1996

Harris A., Jamieson I., Pearce D. and Russ J. (1997), *Effective Teaching and Learning in Work-Related Contexts – Report of a Research Project funded by the Department for Education and Employment 1996/97*, DfEE, London

Hillage J. and Hirsh W. (1996), *Changing work patterns: the implications for careers education and guidance*, Institute of Employment Studies, Brighton

Honey P. and Mumford (1982), *The Manual of Learning Styles*, Peter Honey, Maidenhead

Hooton J. and Turner D. (1997), *Transition Teams*, CCDU Training and Consultancy, Leeds

Hutton W. (1996), *The 30/30/40 society*, RSA Journal, March 1996

Joyce B. and Showers B. (1988), *Student Achievement through Staff Development*, Longman, New York

Killeen J. and Kidd J. (1993), *Learning Outcomes of Guidance: A Review of Recent Research*, Employment Department Research Paper No 85, London: ED.

Kolb D. A. (1984), *Experiential Learning*, Prentice Hall, New Jersey

Law B. (1981), *Community interaction: A mid-range focus for theories of career development in young adults*, British Journal of Guidance and Counselling

Law B. (1991, 1995), *Co-ordinating Careers Work* in Careers Work, Open College

Law B. (1991, 1995), *Community Links* in Careers Work, Open College

Law B. (1996), *Staff Development* in Watts et al (1996), *Rethinking Careers Education and Guidance, Theory, Policy and Practice*, Routledge, London and New York

Law B. (1996), *A Career-learning Theory* in Watts et al (1996), *Rethinking Careers Education and Guidance*, Theory, Policy and Practice, Routledge, London and New York

McNiff J., Lomax P. and Whitehead J. (1996), *You and Your Action Research Project*, Hyde Publications/Routledge, London

Miller A., Watts A. G. and Jamieson I. (1991), *Rethinking Work Experience*, Falmer Press, London

Morris M., Simkin C. and Stoney M. (1995), *The Role of the Careers Service in Careers Education and Guidance in Schools*, NFER/DfEE, London

National Council for Educational Technology (1996), *Evaluating the Impact of IT in Good Practice Guide 4 of the 'Using IT in Careers Education and Guidance' series*, NCET, Coventry

OFSTED (1995), *A survey of careers education and guidance in schools*, HMSO, London

OFSTED (1995), *Guidance on the Inspection of Secondary Schools*, HMSO, London

QADU (1996), *Guidelines to Good Practice in Promoting Equal Opportunities in the Careers Service*, DfEE, London

Richardson W. (ed)(1992), *Work Related Teaching and Learning in Schools – Education and Business in Partnership*, The Centre for Education and Industry, Warwick

Roberts K. (1996), *Recurrent Guidance for Prolonged Transitions* – Paper to A Symposium for Heads, Governors, and Curriculum Managers, May 1996

Roberts K. (1996), *Prolonged Transitions to Uncertain Destinations: The Scope for Careers Work* – Paper given at the Kent Careers Service 'Looking Forward' conference, 28 June 1996

Rogers C. and Farson R. (1976), *Active Listening*, from *Readings in Communication*, Communication for Management.

School Curriculum and Assessment Authority (1995), *Looking Forward*, SCAA, London

Seligman L. (1994), *Developmental Career Counselling and Assessment*, Sage Publications, California

Sharf R. S. (1992), *Applying Career Development Theory to Counselling*, Brooks/Cole Publishing Company, California

Stables A. (1996), *Subjects of Choice – The Process and Management of Pupil and Student Choice*, Cassell, London

Stanford G. and Stoate P. (1991), *Developing Effective Classroom Groups: A practical guide for teachers*, Acora Books, Bristol

Squirrel G. (1995), *Individual Action Plans: A Practical Guide*, David Fulton

Summerson L. (1992), *Careers libraries in the 21st Century*, Trotman

TVEI (1991), *Learners First*, in *Choice for the Future Book 6*, TVEI

Watts A. G. (1991), *Individual Action Planning: Issues and Strategies*, Essex County Council Education Department

Watts A. G., Law B., Killeen J., Kidd J. M. and Hawthorn R. (1996), *Rethinking Careers Education and Guidance*, Routledge, London

Watts A. G., Super D. E. and Kidd J. M. (eds)(1981), *Career Development in Britain – Some contributions to theory and practice*, Careers Research and Advisory Centre (CRAC)/Hobsons, Cambridge

Weston P., Tomlins B., with Stoney S. and Ashby P. (1995), *An Evaluation of the Use Made of Action Plans*, NFER, for the Careers Services Quality Assurance and Development Unit of the Department for Education and Employment, DfEE, London

Whiteside T. (1994), *Tutoring and guidance post-16: the student's view*, The Curriculum Journal, Volume 5, No 3